Dedication

Ten precious grandchildren, candidates for life everlasting—

Vanessa, Vivyan, Emily, Cady, Cliff, Candi,
Britney, Ryan, Randy, Kelli

Other Books by Herbert E. Douglass

How to Survive in the 21st Century
Messenger of the Lord
Should We Ever Say, "I Am Saved"?
Why Jesus Waits

Contents

Foreword

The Bible is full of wonderful stories describing God's dealings with people. At times He gave counsel through His prophets. At other times He gave warnings. If the warnings were heeded, blessings followed, but if they were disregarded, dire consequences resulted. It is clear that our Creator wants nothing but the best for His creatures, yet human stubbornness and unbelief often frustrate God's purposes. Fortunately, over the centuries there were people like Joshua, Daniel, Paul, Naomi, David, and many more who provided proof positive that following God's leading always is best.

In 1903, Ellen White urged that stories recounting God's leading in the early days of the Advent movement be reprinted. In the pages that follow, Dr. Herbert E. Douglass does exactly that, sharing not just the stories but also important insights into the significance of the long-ago events that he narrates.

As God did in Bible days, so in more modern times He sent a prophet to guide and warn those who would listen. This book is full of the sometimes amazing, but at other times tragic, tales of how the founders of the Seventh-day Adventist Church reacted to the counsels God gave through Ellen White. Often they heeded, and they and the movement of which they were a part prospered. Sadly, at other times they refused to listen and be guided, and the results warn us that if we disregard God's instructions today we do so at our own peril.

Each person or event depicted in this book was directly affected by one or more of Ellen White's visions. Names of nearly forgotten individuals, such as Daniel Kress, Hiram Patch, and Nathaniel Faulkhead, plus many more, come alive as their intriguing stories unfold for the reader. In each case, Ellen White, ever the soul winner, is seen at her very best, urging people to change course and thus avoid spiritual ruin. In other stories we catch glimpses of God working through Ellen White to save the denomination as a whole.

Just as we can learn from the study of people and events in Bible times, so we can also learn from the study of people and events in the history of the Advent movement. As the stories in this book amply remind us, the admonition of King Jehoshaphat found in 2 Chronicles 20:20 is as applicable today as when he first uttered it, "Believe in the LORD your God, so shall ye be established; believe his prophets, so shall ye prosper."

James R. Nix, Director
Ellen G. White Estate, Inc.

Introduction

The twenty-four stories contained in this book are a sampling of Ellen White's seventy years of service to the world. However, these stories focus on only one aspect of her seventy-year ministry—her contribution directly to men and women who had anxieties, questions, and problems such as we all have from time to time.

Modern readers have little or no access to these special moments that changed lives forever. However, we today can relive those events and easily role-play with the individuals noted in the following pages. Even in the twenty-first century, we can identify with their circumstances and rejoice with them as they realized how much God thought of them in coming so close to their private lives, either in comfort or in warning.

Years have passed but not the human condition: We have the same dreams, hopes, and frailties as the young and old who live again in these pages.

I have tried to connect these stories to Ellen White's age and her own personal circumstances, showing how she fulfilled her role as God's messenger in her twenties, thirties, etc. Many of these stories are found also in my book *Messenger of the Lord*—but without many of the fascinating details I have been able to include in the present volume.

These stories can be used effectively in family worship, Sabbath School, and sermons. Each one can be the source of much contemplation as we relive each circumstance. Most of these situations are replayed again and again. The principles once given are as fresh as the morning dew today.

None of us has had the privilege of knowing this intrepid church leader personally. We have never heard this five-foot-two woman speak in public, where twenty thousand people, without the aid of a public address system, could hear her. We can only read of her devotion to four children and her beloved husband—and of their adoration for her. But these stories tell us much about the woman who helped shape a world movement.

We hope that in these twenty-four stories we can relive some of Ellen White's remarkable contributions that have changed the lives of many millions in the world who can feel close to her as the Lord's messenger, then and now.

Herbert E. Douglass
Lincoln Hills, CA

Chapter 1

Egg in Grape Juice—Saving Dr. Daniel Kress

*I*n far-off Australia, Dr. Daniel H. Kress was dying—and he was only forty.

After joining the Adventist Church, Kress and his wife, Lauretta, took their medical training together at the University of Michigan. The worked for three years with Dr. John Harvey Kellogg at the Battle Creek Sanitarium before they were called in 1898 to establish medical work in England.

In 1900 they were sent to Australia to develop a medical work there. A year later, Kress was dying. The problem: Kress zealously advocated a vegan diet. Back in Battle Creek, he had been a close follower of Dr. John Harvey Kellogg and his associates. In England and now in Australia, Kress taught consistently that butter, milk, and eggs should be dropped from the diet. Later in life he wrote: "I aimed to practice what I taught. It was difficult for me to get suitable foods in traveling from place to place, and as a result my food was lacking in some essential elements. I ran down in health almost to the point of death."

Now back in California after her nine years in Australia, Ellen White in vision saw Dr. Kress at death's door. In her usual straightforward manner, she instructed him to "make changes at once. Put into your diet something you have left out."

She told him: "Because some are far behind, you must not, in order to be an example to them, be an extremist. . . . Your devotion to true principles is leading you to submit yourself to a diet which is giving you an experience that will not recommend health reform."

Here is Ellen White's vision-based prescription to Kress for regaining his health:

> Get eggs of healthy fowls. Use these eggs cooked or raw. Drop them uncooked into the best unfermented wine you can find. This will supply that which is necessary to your system. Do not for a moment suppose that it will not be right to do this. . . .
>
> We appreciate your experience as a physician, and yet I say that milk and eggs should be included in your diet.

Then she added: "The time will come when milk cannot be used as freely as it is now used; but the present is not the time to discard it. And eggs contain properties which are remedial agencies in counteracting poisons."

What Ellen did not know then—but what we know now—is that Dr. Kress was dying from pernicious anemia, an often fatal disease. His diet, without a wide variety of vegetables and fruit, was lacking in folic acid and vitamins B_6 and B_{12}.

Dr. Kress immediately followed Ellen White's advice to eat eggs and grape juice—and in a few weeks made a quick recovery. He lived fifty-five more years, dying at ninety-four. He returned with his wife to America in 1907 to become the first medical superintendent of the new Washington Sanitarium and Hospital in Takoma Park, Maryland.

He lived fifty-five more years because Ellen White stepped into Kress's life with a message from God.

Kress was one of many men and women whom God gave individual counsel, encouragement, or reproof through His messenger Ellen White. Before we read stories of other individuals who received specific personal counsel from God's messenger, we will review the event—a vision—that launched Ellen's seven decades of service as God's messenger.

Chapter 2

The Vision That Launched a Movement—The Narrow Path

*1*844! What a year! Samuel F. B. Morse transmits the first telegraph message ("What hath God wrought!"). Wood-pulp-paper process is invented, reducing the price of newsprint. A Boston dentist, pioneering anesthesiology with nitrous oxide, extracts his own tooth. Brigham Young is chosen to lead Mormons after Joseph Smith is lynched in Carthage, Illinois. Karl Marx, twenty-six, writes, "Religion is the sigh of the oppressed creature . . . the opium of the people."

And God bends low to talk to seventeen-year-old Ellen Harmon, a near-total invalid, in Portland, Maine, during the first week of December.

A few weeks before, Ellen and approximately one hundred thousand other Methodists, Baptists, and Presbyterians were sadly disappointed when on October 22, 1844, Jesus did not return as they had hoped. She recalled,

> It was a bitter disappointment that fell upon the little flock whose faith had been so strong and whose hope had been so high. But we were surprised that we felt so free in the Lord, and were so strongly sustained by His strength and grace. . . .
> We were disappointed, but not disheartened.

Ellen's precarious health worsened rapidly. Able to speak only in a whisper, she also found it difficult to breathe lying down and was awakened often by coughing and by bleeding from her lungs. Dying from tuberculosis, Ellen was so weak she had to be transported by wheelchair and often was fed by others.

In this condition, she responded to an invitation from a close friend, Mrs. Elizabeth Haines, to visit her and three other women for a prayer meeting in her South Portland home. These women were also confused and disappointed. They had given up confidence in the validity of the October date but they still hoped for Jesus to return sometime in the near future.

We today can remember a similar, bitter disappointment afflicting the disciples after their Lord's crucifixion. How heavy their hearts when Jesus appeared to two of them on the road to Emmaus a few hours after His resurrection. What a difference His presence meant! What a fresh way to look at the future!

So, on that December morning in 1844, our Lord visited those troubled believers with the same kind of encouragement that those troubled believers needed eighteen centuries earlier.

Ellen later recalled: "It was not an exciting occasion. . . . While I was praying, the power of God came upon me as I had never felt it before. I was wrapped in a vision of God's glory, and seemed to be rising higher and higher from the earth, and was shown something of the travels of the Advent people to the Holy City."[1]

Although Ellen recounted this experience and the vision orally, she didn't record it in writing until more than a year later because she could not hold her hand steady enough to hold a pen.

What was the vision that launched her seventy-year ministry, a vision that became more significant as the years went by?

While [I was] praying at the family altar, the Holy Ghost fell upon me, and I seemed to be rising higher and higher, far above the dark world. I turned to look for the Advent people in the world, but could not find them, when a voice said to me, Look again, and look a little higher.

Straight and narrow path

At this, I raised my eyes and saw a straight and narrow path, cast up high above the world. On this path the Advent people were traveling to the city, which was at the farther end of the path. They had a bright light set up behind them at the first end of the path, which an angel told me was the Midnight Cry. This light shone all along the path and gave light for their feet so they might not stumble.

Eyes fixed on Jesus

And if they kept their eyes fixed on Jesus, who was just before them, leading them to the City, they were safe. But soon some grew weary, and said the City was a great way off, and they expected to have entered it before. Then Jesus would encourage them by raising His glorious right arm, and from His arm came a glorious light which waved over the Advent band, and they shouted, Hallelujah!

Some denied the light behind them

Others rashly denied the light behind them and said that it was not God that had led them out so far. The light behind them went out, which left their feet in perfect darkness, and they stumbled and got their eyes off the mark and lost sight of Jesus, and fell off the path down in the dark and wicked world below. It was just as impossible for them to get on the path again and go to the City, as all the wicked world which God had rejected. They fell all the way along the path one after another, until we heard the voice of God like many waters, which gave us the day and hour of Jesus' coming. The living saints, 144,000 in number, knew and understood the voice, while the wicked thought it was thunder and an earthquake. When God spake the time, He poured on us the Holy Ghost, and our faces began to light up and shine with the glory of God as Moses' did when he came down from Mount Sinai.

By this time the 144,000 were all sealed and perfectly united. On their foreheads was written, God, New Jerusalem, and a glorious star containing Jesus' new name.

At our happy, holy state the wicked were enraged, and would rush violently up to lay hands on us to thrust us in prison, when we would stretch forth the hand in the name of the Lord, and the wicked would fall helpless to the ground. Then it was that the synagogue of Satan knew that God had loved us who could wash one another's feet and salute the holy brethren with a holy kiss, and they worshiped at our feet.

Cloud in the east

Soon our eyes were drawn to the east, for a small black cloud had appeared, about half as large as a man's hand, which we all knew was the sign of the Son of man. We all in solemn silence gazed on the cloud as it drew nearer, [and became] lighter, and brighter, glorious, and still more glorious, till it was a great white cloud. The bottom appeared like fire, a rainbow was over it, around the cloud were ten thousand angels singing a most lovely song.

And on it sat the Son of man, on His head were crowns, His hair was white and curly and lay on His shoulders. His feet had the appearance of fire, in His right hand was a sharp sickle, in His left a silver trumpet. His eyes were as a flame of fire, which searched His children through and through.

Who shall be able to stand?

Then all faces gathered paleness, and those that God had rejected gathered blackness. Then we all cried out, Who shall be able to stand? Is my robe spotless? Then the angels ceased to sing, and there was some time of awful silence, when Jesus spoke, Those who have clean hands and a pure heart shall be able to stand; My grace is sufficient for you. At this, our faces lighted up, and joy filled every heart. And the angels struck a note higher and sung again while the cloud drew still nearer the earth.

Then Jesus' silver trumpet sounded, as He descended on the cloud, wrapped in flames of fire. He gazed on the graves of the sleeping saints, then raised His eyes and hands to heaven and cried, Awake! Awake! Awake! ye that sleep in the dust, and arise. Then there was a mighty earthquake. The graves opened, and the dead came up clothed with immortality. The 144,000 shouted, Hallelujah! as they recognized their friends who had been torn from them by death, and in the same moment we were changed and caught up together with them to meet the Lord in the air.[2]

Why did God give this remarkable vision to a Sunday-keeping, dying teenager who could barely whisper?

We can think of many reasons that would tell us something about God Himself and what He thinks about faithful believers wherever they are in their spiritual journey.

God not far from His faithful

Just as He understood the bitter disappointment of those two disciples on the way to Emmaus, He understood the empty sadness of those five young women in Portland, Maine. And He is not far away from the readers of these pages who have had heartbreak and perhaps abandonment.

God knows how to comfort

Those early Adventist believers needed to be comforted. They were confused about what had seemed to be clear biblical truths—their Christian experience seemed to be genuine. They had not given up their confidence in God but were confused nevertheless.

This vision gave those five women—and then a growing group who later caught the highlights of the vision—the intellectual and emotional comfort that their several years of preparation for the return of Jesus in 1844 had not been wasted on theological mischief. They had not been deluded, only confused about what was to happen on October 22. And this assurance that the Lord had been leading them in their past experience could help them better face the ridicule from former friends.

This vision also gave them the assurance that if faithful, they would one day see their Lord face to face. No matter what difficulties might arise, if they continued to follow the light, they, too, would end up on the sea of glass and walk the streets of gold.

God knows how to instruct the faithful

For several years, these five young women had believed that Jesus would return in 1843, then 1844, based on careful biblical research. But, after October 22, they had been sinking deeper into disappointment because Jesus had not come. Their faith began to waver, not in their Christian experience but in their confidence in Bible study.

By December most Advent believers had abandoned their once-solid belief that October 22 mattered. In other words, they believed that the 2,300-day-year prophecy had not ended; worse still, some now believed that the whole prophetic picture had been in error. As Ellen wrote in 1847, "At the time I had the vision of the midnight cry [December 1844], I had given it up in the past and thought it future, as also most of the band had."[3]

But this December vision gave those troubled Advent believers an entirely different picture. God had been leading His people! The unforgettable "Midnight Cry" in the summer of 1844 was now to shine as a light upon the pathway of those who would cheerfully make their way to the heavenly Canaan. The promise: If they would keep trusting that light and keep their eyes fixed on Jesus, they would safely enter into their reward.

What a promise! What a comfort!

What does that vision say to us today?

I remember the day when I read this vision for the first time. I was in my early teens and had just been baptized. Someone thought that I would find *Early Writings* helpful. That Sabbath afternoon is as clear as yesterday. I was lying across my bed reading those remarkable pages, page after page, chapter by chapter.

I didn't know until later that I was being introduced to the great controversy theme and how God is thinking about bringing the history of sin and of this world to its conclusion. My reading that Sabbath afternoon became my first steps in grasping the overarching story of why sin developed and how God is doing His best to tell His side of the story.

"Look a little higher"

The instruction to "look a little higher" became one of the refrains that has helped me through shadow and disappointment ever since. When obvious questions seemed without ready answers, when trusted friends disappointed, the steadying voice lifted my eyes— "look a little higher!"

"Straight and narrow path"

The words "straight and narrow path" bring to mind our Lord's words in Matthew 7:13, 14, where He reminds us that life offers choices. We have one journey to complete, but one can choose the direction. We all know that one does not automatically walk along the straight and narrow path. For whatever reason, we start walking along the easy path, the wide path, with plenty of company. In fact, we don't really know that there is a better path until Jesus and the Holy Spirit turn us around—the U-turn that we call conversion. But that U-turn puts us on a narrower path, a path that keeps calling for choices and decisions as we keep walking.

Unfortunately, some English translations substitute the word *difficult* for *narrow*. Jesus does not contradict Himself. When He says that His "yoke is easy" and His "burden is light" (Matthew 11:30), He is telling us that the Holy Spirit smoothes our paths, enlightens our minds, and empowers our choices—and what devil can match that promise? The difficulty in the Christian's life happens when he or she tries to walk both ways on the road of life at the same time!

"A bright light . . . behind them"

The reference to the bright light behind them shook those five young women and then the growing group of Adventists into seeing the great significance in the events of October 22, 1844. Without that "bright light" called "the Midnight Cry," those disappointed early Adventists would have dug their graves in despair. The midnight cry had been the rallying theme during the summer of 1844, a phrase lifted from the bridegroom parable in Matthew 25. It had united many, many thousands as they focused on October 22. In other words, God was endorsing their unalloyed confidence and commitment in the time prophecy of Daniel 8:14. What a relief! What a reason now to gather themselves together and start the journey on that "narrow path," watching for more light along the way.

"Eyes fixed on Jesus"

Early Adventists were not given the entire picture at once. Such has never been God's plan. Throughout our Lord's earthly ministry, He was leading His disciples along step by step: "I still have many things to say to you, but you cannot bear them now" (John 16:12, NKJV). People cannot relate to too much information or change at once. But what we can do safely is to keep our eyes "fixed on Jesus."

Following this simple instruction, all of us can trace our own walk along the narrow path. The Holy Spirit leads us along at different speeds, depending on intellectual backgrounds, social habits, and family connections. Even devoted husbands and wives are not exactly at the same point on that narrow path. The open secret is to keep reading the written Word, keep associating with others on that narrow path, and never turn back.

"They were safe"

Precious promise! Keep following the light that shines along the path, the light that was anchored in the events of 1844, the light ahead that keeps leading us to the city—and we are safe all along the way! We may not live long enough to walk through the city's gate before resting in the grave, but if we have been steadily walking into the brightening light, we are safe to be given eternal life!

Christian assurance rests on this simple truth—those who are walking in the light they have, not always the light that may be guiding others, always trusting and obeying the light, as they understand more and more—that person has the quiet strength of the assurance of salvation.

"Some grew weary"

Early Adventist believers had hoped that Christ would soon return. The last-day message to the entire world dawned on them slowly, step by step. Some did not perceive quickly that the quality of the last-day church as described in Revelation (2:17; 14:12; 19:7–9) would take time to develop and that development had everything to do with the time of the Advent. Unfortunately, some indeed grew weary, hoping for spiritual shortcuts. Others eventually caught on to God's end-time plans, and they gathered up their strength, choosing to belong to those who followed "the shining light, that shineth more and more unto the perfect day" (Proverbs 4:18). That's what happens when God's loyalists keep their eyes fixed on Jesus.

"Rashly denied the light behind them"

What could this mean? For whatever reason, some rejected the thought that God had been leading the Advent believers. They lost confidence in the 2,300-year prophecy of Daniel 8:14, and their once-eager faith turned to bitterness, thinking that they had been deceived. The light went out and they returned to the fast-fading allurements of this present world.

"Wicked were enraged"

Reality returns. Just as early Adventists had once endured the ridicule and a certain level of rage from those who rejected the Adventists prior to October 22, so last-day Adventists will face the same rage at the end of this world's history, just before the return of Jesus. This time the confrontation will be worldwide and fearsome; their only defense will be the promises of Jesus and the light that has been guiding them. At the bleakest time of these last days, they will get heavenly signals that relief is on the way. Rainbows, white clouds, angelic choruses—it will all be worth it!

"Awful silence"

Could there be a more awe-filled moment in the history of planet Earth? The wicked are stunned beyond words; the righteous raise their humble question, "Who shall be worthy?" No one, not even the most faithful believers, knows that he or she is worthy of meeting Jesus face to face. Then that reassuring voice, which they have "heard" many times in their walk along the narrow path, reminds them that His "grace is sufficient." The simple gospel, full and complete, has reached its grand goal—the good news of pardon and power has led them finally to the feet of their loving and faithful Lord.

"Silver trumpet"

Immediately the early Adventists who heard this vision unfolded remembered the trumpets in 1 Thessalonians 4 when the graves are opened and old friends reunited. No words on earth today can possibly embrace all that the loyal believers of all the ages will be hearing, seeing, and thinking. Our only response to this vision is to re-commit our lives to being there!

Throughout her seventy years of ministry, Ellen White referred to the narrow path metaphor at least 135 times. In the following excerpt from a letter to a young person who was in danger of losing his way, Ellen shows her mental and moral clarity:

I have been shown the dangers of youth. Their hearts are full of high anticipations, and they see the downward road strewn with tempting pleasures which look very inviting; but death is there. The narrow path to life may appear to them to be destitute of attractions, a path of thorns and briers, but it is not. It is the path that requires a denial of sinful pleasures; it is a narrow path, cast up for the ransomed of the Lord to walk in. None can walk this path and carry with them their burdens of pride, self-will, deceit, falsehood, dishonesty, passion, and the carnal lusts. The path is so narrow that these things will have to be left behind by those who walk in it, but the broad road is wide enough for sinners to travel it with all their sinful propensities.

Young man, if you reject Satan with all his temptations you may walk in the footsteps of your Redeemer and have the peace of heaven, the joys of Christ. You cannot be happy in the indulgence of sin. You may flatter yourself that you are happy, but real happiness you cannot know. The character is becoming deformed by the indulgence of sin. Danger is encountered at every downward step, and those who could help the youth do not see or realize it. The kind and tender interest which should be taken in the young is not manifested. Many might be kept from sinful influences if they were surrounded with good associations and had words of kindness and love spoken to them.[4]

This first vision of about two thousand that would follow during the next seventy years set the course for millions of Adventist believers. Its graphic clarity is difficult to forget. No one can read it carefully and ever plead ignorance at the Second Coming.

We today can thank God even as those early Adventists did that He bends low to confused believers even today, shining a light on each person's path. And He continues to show us today how to stay on that narrow path. The light gets brighter and the assurance deepens as we listen for the trumpets and the swish of angel wings as they gather long-separated loved ones for that journey to the Holy City.

---

[1] *Early Writings*, 13.
[2] *The Day-Star*, Jan. 24, 1846 (see also *Early Writings*, 14–16).
[3] Letter 3, 1847.
[4] *Testimonies*, vol. 4, 364.

Chapter 3

Longest Vision and That Heavy Bible—Randolph, Massachusetts

*E*llen White's longest vision (four hours) occurred in 1845, one year before her marriage to James. One of the allegations against her was that she could not have a vision if James White and her sister, Sarah (both persons who had been accompanying Ellen on her early travels), were not present.

Otis Nichols, a Bostonian, hoped to expose these charges. He and his wife "invited Ellen and Sarah to their home, leaving James in Portland. Among those in the Boston area who contested the validity of Ellen Harmon's experiences and visions were fanatical leaders, including Sargent and Robbins, who were also advocating that it was a sin to work."

Sargent and Robbins's message to the Millerite Adventists was, "Sell that ye have, and give alms," meaning, of course, to pay them their living expenses. They argued that they were now in the "jubilee, the land should rest and the poor must be supported without labor." They denounced Ellen Harmon's early visions as "being of the devil" because she had been exposing their errors.

A few days after Ellen and Sarah had arrived at the Nichols's home, Sargent and Robbins were invited to come and share Bible studies and prayer. When they arrived and learned that the two sisters were in the house, they hastily departed amidst a flurry of excuses.

But before they left, Nichols told the two men that Ellen wanted to attend the meeting with their "No Work" group in Boston on the following Sabbath (Sunday). When he asked if the two leaders had objections to hearing her testimony, they replied, "None at all. Let her come next Sabbath."

So, the arrangements were made for Ellen and Sarah Harmon to attend this group meeting on the next Sunday. "But the night before the proposed meeting, Ellen was shown in vision that these men had no plan to meet with her; they had alerted their followers to gather in Randolph, thirteen miles south of Boston. In that vision she also was told that she should meet with this group in Randolph, that God would give her a message that would convince 'the honest, the unprejudiced ones, whether her visions were of the Lord or from Satan.' "

When Ellen, Sarah, and the Nichols family arrived the next day in Randolph, they found a large room full of people in the Thayer home. Ellen wrote later: "As we entered, Robbins and Sargent looked at each other in surprise and began to groan. They had promised to meet me in Boston, but thought they would disappoint us by going to Randolph, and while we were in Boston, warn the brethren against us."

During the morning meeting, "Robbins told Sarah . . . that Ellen could not have a vision if he were present! In the afternoon meeting" Ellen had the vision that supposedly could not happen. She reported later:

> The blessing of the Lord rested upon me, and I was taken off in vision. I was again shown the errors of these wicked men and others united with them. I saw that they could not prosper, their errors would confuse and distract; some would be deceived by them; but that truth would triumph in the end, and error be brought down.
>
> I was shown that they were not honest, and then I was carried into the future and shown that they would continue to despise the teachings of the Lord, to despise reproof, and that they would be left in total darkness, to resist God's Spirit until their folly should be made manifest to all. A chain of truth was presented to me from the Scriptures, in contrast with their errors.

When I came out of vision, candles were burning. I had been in vision nearly four hours.

Otis Nichols recorded that when Ellen began to pray, she soon was "taken off in vision . . . and continued talking in vision with a shrill voice which could be distinctly understood by all present, until about sundown."

One can easily understand the consternation and exasperation of Sargent, Robbins, and others. How did they respond? Nichols said that these embarrassed leaders "exhausted all their influence and bodily strength to destroy the effect of the vision. They would unite in singing very loud, and then alternately would talk and read from the Bible in a loud voice in order that Ellen might not be heard, until their strength was exhausted and their hands would shake, so they could not read from the Bible."

Some of the followers of these humiliated leaders rebuked them, asking them to stop their interference. Robbins responded, "You are bowed to an idol. You are worshiping a golden calf."

Mr. Thayer, the owner of the house, had his own way of satisfying himself as to whether the vision was of the devil. He had heard that placing an open Bible on the person in vision could stop people under satanic influence. Thayer asked Sargent to lay a Bible on Ellen, but he declined.

Thayer went further. He "took a heavy, large quarto family Bible which was lying on the table and seldom used, opened it, and laid it open upon the breast of Ellen while in vision, as she was then inclined backward against the wall in one corner of the room." This is what happened next:

> Immediately after the Bible was laid upon her, she arose upon her feet and walked into the middle of the room, with the Bible open in one hand and lifted up as high as she could reach, and with her eyes steadily looking upward, declared in a solemn manner, "The inspired testimony of God," or words of the same import, and then she continued for a long

time, while the Bible was extended in one hand and her eyes [were] looking upward and not on the Bible, to turn over the leaves with the other hand and place her finger upon certain passages and correctly utter their words with a solemn voice.

If you had been in that room, what would you have done? Exactly what many did! They stood and looked at those biblical texts to which Ellen was pointing while her eyes were looking upward. To their astonishment, she was quoting those texts perfectly.

What were some of those texts? Nichols said that "some of the passages referred to were judgments against the wicked and blasphemous; and others were admonitions and instructions relative to our present condition.

"In this state she continued all the afternoon until nearly sundown when she came out of vision."

When Ellen came out of vision, Sargent, Robbins, and their group were silent. For the remainder of the time they were troubled yet defiant, refusing to acknowledge the significance of what they had experienced.

What became of Sargent, Robbins and their "No Work" party? Nichols reported that a few weeks later, Ellen Harmon visited Randolph for the last time and told the group that she had learned from her visions that the "curse of God would soon follow their course."

And thus it did! In a few weeks, the group broke up with some confessing "most shameful acts" and the honest-hearted separating for good. About twenty followed Sargent and Robbins, continuing to denounce Ellen Harmon's visions and those who objected to their "No Work" doctrines. A year later, even this group disintegrated, many "declaring themselves free from all sinning!"

It was quite a responsibility for eighteen-year-old Ellen to go toe-to-toe with strong-willed men, not just one at a time but with a roomful of defiant, ridiculing adults! But when a person, regardless of age, has seen the light of truth, no devil or stiff-necked man or woman can crowd out that light.

What about the few who stood by Ellen that long day watching her "longest vision"? Do you think that they ever forgot Ellen and that eighteen- to twenty-pound Bible held aloft for so long? Or her perceptive descriptions of the kind of opposition that so hypocritically denounced her? Or her blazing prediction that this "No Work" party would soon disintegrate in their own sins?

They learned early that it is always safer to "believe His prophets" (2 Chronicles 20:20, NKJV).

Chapter 4

The Astronomy Lesson— Bates Was Convinced

Joseph Bates, a converted sea captain, spent his fortune promoting the Millerite message. He became one of the first Sabbatarian Adventists (1845) and the first to print a tract on the seventh-day Sabbath, *The Seventh-day Sabbath Perpetual Sign* (1846). This tract became significant confirmation for James and Ellen White, recently married, that Saturday, not Sunday, is the Christian Sabbath.

However, the sea captain was not at first convinced that Ellen White's visions "were of God." Visions at that time were confused with spiritualistic séances or mesmerism. Bates thought the visions were the result of Ellen's poor health: "nothing 'more than what was produced by a protracted debilitated state of her body.' But he changed his mind after observing her in several vision experiences.

"One vision, in particular, impressed him. In November 1846, at the Stockbridge Howland home in Topsham, Maine, a small company of Sabbath keepers had convened. Among them were Joseph Bates and the Whites. Ellen White was taken in vision and 'for the first time had a view of other planets.' After the vision, she related what she had seen" during the vision. J. N. Loughborough recounted in print the description of the meeting as Bates told it to him:

> Mrs. White, while in vision, began to talk about the stars, giving a glowing description of rosy-tinted belts which she saw across the surface of some planet, and added, "I see four moons."

"Oh," said Elder Bates, "she is viewing Jupiter!"

Then having made motions as though traveling through space, she began giving a description of belts and rings in their ever-varying beauty, and said, "I see seven moons."

Elder Bates exclaimed, "She is describing Saturn."

Next came the description of Uranus, with its six moons; then a wonderful description of the "opening heavens," with its glory, calling it an opening into a region more enlightened. Elder Bates said that her description far surpassed any account of the opening heavens he had ever read from any author.

While she was talking and still in vision, he arose to his feet, and exclaimed, "O how I wish Lord John Rosse was here tonight!" Elder White inquired, "Who is Lord John Rosse?"

"Oh," said Elder Bates, "he is the great English astronomer. I wish he were here to hear that woman talk astronomy, and to hear that description of the 'opening heavens.' It is ahead of anything I ever read on the subject."

Later Ellen White reported of this experience . . . in the Curtis home:

> After I came out of vision I related what I had seen. Elder Bates then asked if I had studied astronomy. I told him I had no recollection of ever looking into an astronomy.
>
> Said he, "This is of the Lord."
>
> I never saw him as free and happy before. His countenance shone with the light of heaven, and he exhorted the church with power.

A few months later James White wrote his recollection of this "astronomy vision":

> At our conference in Topsham, Maine, last November, Ellen had a vision of the handiworks of God. She was guided to the planets Jupiter, Saturn, and I think one more. After she came out of vision, she could give a clear description of their moons,

et cetera. It is well known that she knew nothing of astronomy, and could not answer one question in relation to the planets, before she had this vision.

In reviewing this vision as reported by John Loughborough and James White, we must recognize at least seven facts:

1. Ellen White never wrote out this "astronomy vision."
2. She never identified by name the planets she saw.
3. She never mentioned the number of moons any planet may have.
4. Bates attached the planets' names *to what he thought* Ellen White was describing.
5. Loughborough and James White *reported what Bates seemed to have understood* from her brief comments.
6. Telescopes today reveal much more about the planets, the number of their moons, and other heavenly phenomena than Bates could ever have dreamed of.
7. What really astounded Bates was not the description of "planets" but Mrs. White's description of the "opening heavens," a reference to the so-called "open space in Orion" which, for Bates, "surpassed" any description made by contemporary astronomers.

So what is the point of this vision? This "astronomy vision" was not a lesson on astronomy that would later be verified by the Hubble telescope.

But, "if Ellen White had given a preview of what the Hubble telescope revealed in the 1990s, Joseph Bates would certainly have been convinced that Ellen White was a fraud, a misguided zealot. His doubts would have been confirmed. Probably he would not have identified himself further with Seventh-day Adventists."

In other words, this interesting "astronomy vision" corresponded to Bates's knowledge of what telescopes showed in 1846. Almost certainly this vision was given in Bates's presence to give him confidence in Ellen White's ministry.

And the vision was another example of how God leads His people along "step by step." It was the method of Jesus: "I still have many things to say to you, but you cannot bear them now" (John 16:12, NKJV). People cannot relate to too much change at once. The step-by-step principle applies to a wide variety of issues, including health reform, unfolding of truth such as when to begin the Sabbath, and the development of Loma Linda University Medical Center.

Chapter 5

"Wait a Month!"— Hiram Patch

*T*he time was late winter, 1850. Ellen, just past her twenty-third birthday, was the mother of two sons, Henry, three and one-half, and Edson, six months old.

James White, now about twenty-nine, was holding meetings in Oswego, New York, while writing the copy for the first Seventh-day Adventist missionary journal. He had stirred up the Methodists in town, who were now holding their own meetings. Their speaker, the county treasurer, also served as the Methodist lay preacher.

During this period, two young, unconverted people, twenty-one-year-old Hiram Patch and his fiancée, attended both series of meetings. Eventually, they came to the Whites in their confusion as to whom to believe. During that visit, Ellen White had a vision that they witnessed. She referred the couple to Hosea 5:6, 7: "They shall go with their flocks and with their herds to seek the LORD; but they shall not find him; he hath withdrawn himself from them. They have dealt treacherously against the LORD: for they have begotten strange children: now shall a month devour them with their portions."

Then she told the young couple, "Wait and see the result of the matter. . . . Wait a month, and you will know for yourself the character of the persons who are engaged in this revival, and who profess to have such a great burden for sinners."

Hiram said, "I will wait."

Two weeks later, the treasurer broke a blood vessel in his stomach while screeching during one of his prayers. He was carried home and confined to his bed. The sheriff and the constable took over the county's finances and found a shortage of an even thousand dollars. They went to the treasurer's home, hoping to get some help. But he and his wife raised their hands toward heaven, calling God to witness that they knew nothing of the missing money.

However, when the sheriff went in the front door, his constable had gone to the back of the house and hid in a shed. Suddenly the back door opened, and the wife hurriedly buried a sack in a snowdrift. Moments later, while the sheriff and the treasurer were discussing the discrepancy, the constable marched into the bedroom with the missing money. The treasurer's evangelistic revival suddenly collapsed, and Hiram Patch and his soon-to-be wife made their choice to join the Sabbath-keeping Adventists. They remained loyal members till their deaths.

What do we learn in this little incident? Ellen White was forever a soul winner! God gave her a vision that helped to bring two young people into the safety of biblical truth. At the same time, God gave two hypocrites a chance to make things right, but they rejected their opportunity to come clean.

Chapter 6

"Another Rebel Has Surrendered!"— Stephen Smith

*I*n November 1851, even though Ellen White was not quite twenty-four, she was already involved in helping to settle divergent views of strong-minded men. The emerging Seventh-day Adventist Church was gaining members, and the need for church organization was obvious.

One of the reasons for this early emphasis on church order was a reaction to the destructive work of Stephen Smith, of Unity, New Hampshire (a few miles from Washington, New Hampshire, where the first Seventh-day Adventist church building still stands). One issue was Smith's refusal to accept the counsel that believing a prophetic date for Christ's second coming was no longer a prerequisite for church membership. Smith picked up other nonbiblical ideas and then joined the opposition to the Whites and other church leaders.

Ellen had a vision concerning the unrest and saw that the church must act to confine the errors and dissension by disfellowshiping Stephen Smith and others promoting erroneous teachings. James White reported in his general letter of November 11: "At Washington we met Brother Smith, *hard, hard,* full of errors." "It was a battle. . . . Sunday, Brother Smith was present. Hard as ever. We talked plain. Finally the conference voted to withdraw from him."

"About a year after he was disfellowshiped, Stephen Smith came to see his errors, confessed, and was restored into fellowship." But soon "he again became involved in erroneous views and was again disfellowshiped. In 1857 he again found his way back, but only for a short time.

"At some point in the 1850s, after one of his lapses, Ellen White wrote him a testimony in which she depicted what his life would be if he persisted in the course he was following. When he received the letter, he feared that it was a testimony of reproof, . . . so he . . . tucked it deep in a trunk, still unopened and unread."

For nearly thirty years Stephen Smith continued to oppose his former denomination with mean and cutting criticism. "Mrs. Smith remained faithful, and the *Review and Herald,* the Seventh-day Adventist church paper, came weekly to their home. Then one day Smith picked it up and read an article from Ellen White. He continued to read her weekly articles and found they spoke to his heart." Eventually, his attitude began to soften.

In 1885 E. W. Farnsworth returned to Washington, New Hampshire, to hold revival meetings. Eugene's father was William Farnsworth, a charter member of the first Adventist church at Washington, New Hampshire. Stephen Smith had known Eugene as a boy, and he now walked twelve miles to hear his Sabbath sermon. Farnsworth preached on the rise and development of the Adventist Church. "The sermon over, Smith rose to his feet and asked for the privilege of speaking. The audience, who knew him well, expected a . . . blast of criticism and meanness.

" 'I don't want you to be afraid of me, brethren,' " Smith began. " 'I have not come to criticize you. I have quit that kind of business.' Then he reviewed the past, his hatred of church organization, his joining one opposition party after another, which he had seen go down and their sympathizers come to confusion. 'Facts,' said he, 'are stubborn things, but the facts are that those who have opposed this work have come to naught, while those who have been in sympathy with it have prospered, have grown better, more devoted and Godlike. Those who have opposed it have learned only to fight and debate. They have lost all their religion.

" 'No honest man can help seeing that God is with them and against us. I want to be in fellowship with this people in heart and in the church.' Smith intended to stay over in Washington for the meeting on the following Sabbath, but on Wednesday, he thought of the letter from Ellen White in his trunk at home. Feeling he could not wait to read it, he started out early Thursday morning and trudged the twelve miles home and soon had the unopened envelope in his hands. He tore it open and read its contents.

"Back again in Washington on Sabbath he heard Farnsworth preach on the Spirit of Prophecy in the remnant church. When the sermon was over he was on his feet again. Here is what he said: 'I received a testimony myself twenty-eight years ago. I took it home and locked it up in my trunk, and I never read it till last Thursday.' " He explained that all those years he did not read it, "fearing it would make him mad. 'But,' said he, 'I was mad all the time, nearly.' Finally, he said:

Brethren, every word of the testimony for me is true, and I accept it. And I have come to that place where I finally believe they [the testimonies] all are of God, and if I had heeded the one God sent to me as well as the rest, it would have changed the whole course of my life, and I should have been a very different man.

Any man that is honest must say that they lead a man toward God and the Bible always. If he is honest, he will say that; if he won't say that, he is not honest.

If I had heeded them, they would have saved me a world of trouble. The testimonies said there was to be no more "definite time" preached after the '44 movement, but I thought that I knew as much as an old woman's visions, as I used to term it. May God forgive me! But to my sorrow, I found the visions were right, and the man who thought he knew it all was all wrong, for I preached the time in 1854, and spent all I had when if I had heeded them, I should have saved myself all that and much more. The testimonies are right and I am wrong.

"After talking for some time, he concluded, 'Brethren, I am too old to undo what I have done. I am too feeble to get out to our large meetings, but I want you to tell our people everywhere that another rebel has surrendered.'

"A real change took place in Stephen Smith's life and experience, and he was remembered in his later years as a kind, sweet, whole-hearted Seventh-day Adventist."

For many reasons, it doesn't pay to ignore a plain message from the Lord—either in the 1850s or in the twenty-first century.

Chapter 7

"God Knows My Heart!"— The Lying Evangelist

*T*he place: Vergennes, Michigan. Ellen White was twenty-six, James thirty-two. In late May 1853, the Whites were making their first trip into Michigan; their home was still in Rochester, New York. Battle Creek was not yet an Adventist center. At Tyrone, Michigan, Ellen had a vision that related to several companies of Sabbath keepers that she, of course, had not yet met.

One portion of the vision related to a woman professing great holiness who was endeavoring to introduce herself to the new believers in Michigan. All Ellen knew about her was revealed in that Tyrone vision given just after she and James had just entered the state. M. E. Cornell, a young man who had newly embraced the third angel's message, had met the woman a few days before the Whites reached Michigan, but he did not mention her to them. When he learned of what Ellen White had written of the situation, he told Elder Loughborough, with whom he was holding evangelistic meetings: "Now we will watch, and see how the case comes out." He would not tell Loughborough where the woman lived.

When Ellen White asked Cornell about the matter, he replied, "If there is such a woman you will probably find her, as you have appointments where you will be apt to see most, if not all, of the Sabbath keepers in the State."

Loughborough wrote later:

In Sister White's written description of the woman she not only told the woman's mode of procedure, but also that when she should be reproved, she would put on a sanctimonious look, and say, "God—knows—my—heart." She said this woman was traveling about the country with a young man, while her own husband, an old man, was at home working to support them in their evil course. Mrs. White said the Lord had shown her that "notwithstanding all the woman's pretensions to holiness, she and the young man were guilty of violating the seventh commandment."

With this description of the woman in his pocket, Loughborough waited with curiosity to see how the case would turn out.

On June 11 they reached the home where they were to be entertained at Vergennes. Loughborough recalled what happened:

As we alighted from the carriage, and were standing under a large apple tree in front of the house, Sister White said to her husband, "James, we have got to go to the church where that woman lives whom I saw in the Tyrone vision." "Why," said Brother White, "this is not the house where she lives, is it?" "No," said Sister White, "but I saw this man and woman in connection with the case. The woman in this house has no confidence in that woman, but the man here thinks she is all right."

Loughborough continued:

I thought that was a plain venture in the matter, as there had been no exchange of words between Sister White and these persons on the subject.

As we still stood under the tree, Elder Cornell spoke and said, "Brother Brigham is coming." Sister White looked up, while they were still some ten rods off, and said, "Oh! I saw them in connection with this case. None of that load have any confidence in that woman's pretensions."

Then another load drove up. As she looked at them, she said, "That load is divided on the case. Those on the front seat have no confidence in the woman; those on the back seat think she is all right." Then a third load came up. She said, "They are all under the woman's influence."

She then said, "This must be the church where that woman lives; for I have seen all these persons in connection with that affair."

"Sabbath morning the meeting was held in a large barn three miles beyond the home where the visitors were entertained." Loughborough recalled:

While Brother White was preaching, an old man, a young man, and a woman came in. The two former sat down directly in front of Brother White, while the woman took a seat close to the barn door. After a brief discourse from Brother White, Sister White arose to speak. She introduced her remarks by speaking of the care ministers should have that they mar not the work committed to them. She said God could not call a woman to travel about the country with some other man than her husband.

Finally she said, "That woman who just sat down near the door claims that God has called her to preach. She is traveling with this young man who just sat down in front of the desk, while this old man, her husband—God pity him!—is toiling at home to earn means which they are using to carry on their iniquity. She professes to be very holy—to be sanctified. With all her pretensions and talk about holiness, God has showed me that she and this young man have violated the seventh commandment."

All in that barn knew that Sister White had never personally seen these individuals until they came into that barn. Her picking out of the persons and her delineation of the case had weight in favor of her vision.

"Now all eyes turned toward the woman in question, a Mrs. Alcott. What would be her reaction to this plain delineation of her strange witness and her adultery?"
Loughborough continued:

After sitting about one minute, she slowly arose to her feet, put on a sanctimonious look, and said, "God—knows—my—heart." That was all she said, and sat down. Here was just what the Lord showed (May 28) that the woman would say. On June 11 she did just as it was said she would do, and said the identical words predicted she would say when reproved, and no more.

"During the next few weeks opposition grew that led the young man in the case to return to Canada. Before he left, he was asked by one of the Adventists if Ellen White's vision concerning him was true. He replied, 'That vision was too true.' "

When a prophet is in our midst, "Be sure your sins will find you out." What would happen in any of our churches today if Ellen White should arrive, take the platform, and look around?

Chapter 8

The Waukon Dash—
Reclaiming Two Tired
Preachers

Could the Mississippi River be crossed? Some said No and some said Maybe, but no one said Yes! A vision made the difference.

On the first weekend of December 1856, Ellen, now twenty-nine, and James, thirty-five, were in Round Grove, Illinois, to meet with Adventist believers, some of whom they had known in New England. "This was a time when 'the West' was opening up to settlers." When compared to New England, the fertile land on both sides of the Mississippi River was compared to heaven. Many Adventists had said Goodbye to the rocky farms of New England, where poverty was pervasive, and had followed the call of the rich prairies. Among those who had gone west were the Andrews, Stevens, and Loughborough families—some of the strong Adventist leaders.

For example, the Loughboroughs, at age twenty-five, had spent 1856 holding tent meetings in the evenings and working during the day at jobs such as haying and harvesting, struggling to earn an average of four or five dollars per week. After the fall settlement, Mary Loughborough said, "This is too much; we can't live any longer in this way." John had been a cabinetmaker, and he told Mary that they would go to Waukon and rejoin John Andrews and his family, who were already in Iowa.

In Iowa, they found that Andrews, already the best Adventist theologian at age twenty-eight, was very ill. John Loughborough, discouraged and weary after a year of holding tent meetings, had little energy to help restore the wavering families who were buying up more land and working hard, following the lure of prosperity.

Now, back to Round Grove, Illinois: On December 9, Ellen White had a vision: "I was shown that the company of brethren at Waukon, Iowa, needed help; that Satan's snare must be broken, and these precious souls rescued. My mind could not be at ease until we had decided to visit them."

But the Midwestern winter had set in, and "the Mississippi River had to be crossed, either by boat or on the ice." The Whites were staying with the Harts and the Everts, other former New England families. These two men had learned to trust Ellen's convictions, and they were impressed to take the Whites to Waukon by sleigh.

Ellen White tells the story:

It was then good sleighing, and preparations were made to go with two horses and a sleigh; but as it rained for twenty-four hours, and the snow was fast disappearing, my husband thought the journey must be given up. Yet my mind could not rest; it was agitated concerning Waukon.

Brother Hart said to me, "Sister White, what about Waukon?" I said, "We shall go." "Yes," he replied, "if the Lord works a miracle."

Many times that night I was at the window watching the weather, and about daybreak there was a change, and it commenced snowing. The next evening, about five o'clock, we started on our way to Waukon. . . . Arriving at Green Vale, Illinois, we held meetings with the brethren there.

But at Green Vale another "severe snowstorm struck, delaying the journey nearly a week. On Monday, December 15, James White reported [in the church paper], 'We hope to be able to break through, and pursue our journey . . . in a few days.'[1] In his next report he told of their continued journey as the roads opened, and how as they stopped at the hotels they held meetings introducing the third angel's message. But they had to turn down invitations to hold meetings in the villages. Their mission, he wrote, was 'to visit brethren and sisters who had moved from Maine, Massachusetts, Vermont, and New York, about thirty in number.' . . .

"As they neared the Mississippi River they made many inquiries about crossing. No one thought it could be done. The horses were breaking through the crusted snow at almost every step. The ice on the river was mostly composed of snow, and there was about a foot of water flowing over it. Ellen White recounted the breathtaking experience:

> When we came to the river, Brother Hart arose in the sleigh and said, 'Is it Iowa, or back to Illinois?'. . . .
>
> We answered, 'Go forward, trusting in Israel's God.'
>
> We ventured upon the ice, praying as we went, and were carried safely across. As we ascended the bank on the Iowa side of the river, we united in praising the Lord. A number of persons told us, after we had crossed, that no amount of money would have tempted them to venture upon the ice, and that several teams had broken through, the drivers barely escaping with their lives."

After spending the Sabbath with church members in Dubuque, six miles from the crossing, they moved on to Waukon, still four days' sleighing away.

Ellen wrote: "I never witnessed such cold weather. The brethren would watch each other to see if they were freezing; and we would often hear, 'Brother, your face is freezing, you had better rub the frost out as soon as possible.' 'Your ear is freezing'; or 'Your nose is freezing.' "

Obviously, "Ellen found little time to write, but on Wednesday as they neared Waukon, she got off a little note addressed 'Dear Friends at Home':

> Here we are fourteen miles this side of Waukon. We are all quite well. Have had rather tedious time getting thus far. Yesterday for miles there was no track. Our horses had to plow through snow, very deep, but on we came.

O such fare as we have had on this journey. Last Monday we could get no decent food and tasted not a morsel with the exception of a small apple from morn till night. We have most of the time kept very comfortable, but it is the bitterest cold weather we ever experienced."

After reaching Waukon "she wrote:

We reached Waukon Wednesday night, and found nearly all the Sabbathkeepers sorry that we had come. Much prejudice existed against us, for much had been said concerning us calculated to injure our influence. [In Iowa at that time, The Messenger Party, led by former ministers J. M. Stephenson and D. P. Hall, had raised many allegations against the Whites.] We knew that the Lord had sent us, and that He would there take the work into His own hands.

"Years later Loughborough gave a vivid description of the meeting of the travelers with the believers in Waukon:

As Brother Hosea Mead and I were working on a store building in Waukon, a man looking up saw me, and inquired, 'Do you know a carpenter around here by the name of Hosea Mead?'

I replied, 'Yes, sir, he is up here working with me.'

Brother Mead said, 'That is Elon Everts' voice.' Then he came and looked down, and Brother Everts said, 'Come down; Brother and Sister White and Brother Hart are out here in the sleigh.'

As I reached the sleigh, Sister White greeted me with the question 'What *doest* thou here, Elijah?'

Astonished at such a question, I replied, 'I am working with Brother Mead at carpenter work.'

The second time she repeated, 'What doest *thou* here, Elijah?'

Now I was so embarrassed at such a question, and the connecting of my case with Elijah, that I did not know what to say. It was evident that there was something back of all this which I should hear more about.

The third time she repeated the question, '*What* doest thou here, *Elijah?*'

I was brought by these bare questions to very seriously consider the case of Elijah, away from the direct work of the Lord, hid in a cave. . . . The salutation most thoroughly convinced me that there was going to come a change, and a '*go-back*' from the labor in which I was then engaged."

James and Ellen White spent Sabbath and Sunday meeting with the discouraged believers, discussing the application of the Laodicean message. During "one of the meetings Ellen White was taken off in vision, and in vision solemnly repeated the words 'Return unto me, and I will return unto you, saith the Lord.' These words brought consolation and hope . . . [to] Mary Loughborough, who . . . had been left at home alone while her husband was away preaching, and she was tempted to murmur." In a powerful testimony, "she confessed her bitterness of spirit . . . and urged her husband to return to his ministry.

"At another meeting, John Andrews renewed his consecration to God and to service in the Lord's cause." Every member of the group accepted the encouragement and rebuke, and their focus on serving the Lord, instead of on achieving prosperity, was reestablished.

James and Ellen's long, dangerous winter journey in an open sleigh to spend a few days in Waukon was most profitable. Think about it! Besides reestablishing a growing church in Iowa, two special leaders in the development of the Adventist Church were reclaimed. John Andrews, after he regained his health, returned to Battle Creek. He became a remarkable Bible student and historian and was the first overseas missionary sent by the Seventh-day Adventist Church. Today, we remember this man who turned his back on the possibility of making a fortune in Iowa when we think of Andrews University. John Loughborough returned with his valiant wife and entered a distinguished career as president of five conferences, treasurer of the General Conference, church planter in many fields, and author of several books that are prized today.

Never again did those two men waver. Trial and blessing, perplexities and providences were still ahead—but they never turned back. At one of the Waukon meetings, young Loughborough rose and said: "I have laid up my hammer! I have driven the last nail! Henceforth my hand shall hold the sword of the Spirit, and never give it up. So help me, God!"

Ellen White knew the value of men and women. The winter trip to Waukon was just one example of the danger and inconvenience she would endure to encourage weary and disheartened believers, in this case two young preachers with great potential. Danger that even included crossing the Mississippi River by sleigh in the middle of winter!

---

[1]*Review and Herald,* Jan. 1, 1857.

Chapter 9

Young Preacher Finally Satisfied—Daniel Bourdeau

While still a teenager, Daniel Bourdeau was doing missionary work in Canada for the Baptists when he heard that his parents and older brother (Augustin C.) had joined the Sabbatarian Adventists in northern Vermont.

Even though Daniel did his best to dissuade his family from following the Adventists, they ended up persuading him regarding the Sabbath and other doctrines. But Daniel remained an "unbeliever in the visions." That unbelief transformed into certainty on Sunday, June 21, 1857, when he observed Ellen White in vision at Buck's Bridge, New York. Daniel was given permission to examine Ellen during the vision. This is his report:

> To satisfy my mind as to whether she breathed or not, I first put my hand on her chest sufficiently long to know that there was no more heaving of the lungs than there would have been had she been a corpse. I then took my hand and placed it over her mouth, pinching her nostrils between my thumb and forefinger, so that it was impossible for her to exhale or inhale air, even if she had desired to do so. I held her thus with my hand about ten minutes, long enough for her to suffocate under ordinary circumstances; she was not in the least affected by this ordeal.
>
> Since witnessing this wonderful phenomenon, I have not once been inclined to doubt the divine origin of her visions.*

A year later, Daniel was ordained. Keeping his priorities straight, he spent the next three years looking for a wife. In 1861 he married Marion Saxby in Bakersfield, Vermont. The ceremony took place in a private home with James White officiating.

"Because the service was late in the day, the newlyweds accepted the invitation of their host to spend their wedding night in his home. The Whites also stayed as houseguests.

"When Ellen White went upstairs to retire, she saw a very nervous young man pacing back and forth in front of a closed bedroom door. She suspected a problem. Gently she said to the young bridegroom (as the bride later quoted her husband's recital of the incident): 'Daniel, inside that room is a frightened young woman in bed petrified with fear. Now you go in to her right now, and you love her, and you comfort her. And, Daniel, you treat her gently, and you treat her tenderly, and you treat her lovingly. It will do her good.'

"Then she added, 'Daniel, it will do you good, too!' Here is a Victorian woman who had her priorities straight—and that young couple" was immensely grateful ever after.

Daniel had good reasons to trust Ellen White. A year later, in 1862, he wrote an article for the church paper, *Review and Herald*, that answered some of the basic questions that people sometimes raise against women being given visions, as well as against women speaking in church. He ended his study with this appeal: "We have these productions which we consider as sacred, and before we consent to reject them, our opponents will have to present palpable proofs that they are spurious."

In 1868 Daniel left for California with J. N. Loughborough, responding to a plea from a group of Adventists in San Francisco. The two began the organized work of the Seventh-day Adventist Church in California. In 1870 he returned to the East, resuming work among French-speaking as well as English audiences. He organized churches in Wisconsin and Illinois. Then in 1882, he and his brother, A. C., left for seven years of evangelistic work in Europe, including France, Switzerland, Corsica, Italy, and Alsace-Lorraine.

Daniel finished his ministerial career as a noted preacher and writer—forever mindful of his personal experiences with God's messenger, who illuminated the Bible in a fresh way. A first-hand witness is truth's best evidence—and the ripple effect of that witness rolls on forever.

---

*Bordeau did not base his confidence in Ellen White on physical phenomena only, nor should anyone else. After all, Satan has supernatural powers, and he can counterfeit all of the physical phenomena that are usually associated with prophets, either in the Bible or in the life of Ellen White. The Seventh-day Adventist Church has always maintained that physical phenomena may be evidence of the prophetic gift, but not necessarily proof that any particular phenomenon is from the Lord.

Chapter 10

Tender Letter to a Young Man With Addictions— Victory Jones

*E*llen White talked to audiences large and small, often to care-worn church leaders dealing with major administrative or personnel problems. But she also made time to write hundreds of letters to individual young people who were struggling with personal problems.

Victory Jones was one of those young men who heard from God's messenger. In 1861, Ellen White was thirty-four and very busy with extensive travel. But she had time for Victory Jones, a member in the Monterey, Michigan, church, who was addicted to tobacco and alcohol.

He received a letter that included these words: "If you had left off tobacco entirely and never touched that filthy weed after you had started the last time, your appetite for strong drink you could the more readily have subdued."

After more counsel, she closed her letter with this heartfelt appeal, making a play on his name:

> I have tried to write you what has been shown me. Now, dear friend, I appeal to you, will you take hold of this encouragement which the Lord now presents to you? Will you lay hold upon the hope the Lord now gives you? We feel deeply for you. We cannot leave you to perish. We want you to go with us.
>
> We will pray for you. Pray and watch yourself. Seek for the power of truth in the soul. A mere theory of truth will never

strengthen you to overcome your strong habits. Everlasting life is before you. For the sake of gratifying a depraved appetite, do not make your family wretched, and shut out all happiness from them and be miserable yourself and in the end receive the wages of sin, which is death. . . .

I must close. My prayer is that you may prove worthy of your name. Be an overcomer and walk with Jesus in light because you shall be found worthy, washed and made white in His blood.*

How would you like to receive such a letter of encouragement when you are facing an overwhelming temptation? You can receive the same help Victory did—just by putting your name on this letter.

---

*Letter 1, 1861.

Chapter 11

"No Business in the Desk"— The Bigamist Preacher

Not all of Ellen White's messages were given privately, person to person. Sometimes, they had to be made public for the good of all involved. But not so good for the two-timing, cheating preacher in the pulpit at the Wisconsin camp meeting in 1870.

The preacher "had already begun [his sermon] when the Whites arrived [at the tent]. Ellen and James paused as she said something to James. . . . Those closest heard James say, 'All right!' Down the center aisle they went but Ellen White did not sit down. She looked up at the preacher, pointed her finger at him and said, 'Brother, I have heard your voice in vision, and when I entered this tent this morning, I recognized that voice, and the Lord told me when I heard that voice, to look straight up and deliver the message that He gave me for you and I will have to do it.'

"The preacher stopped. Ellen White continued: 'Brother, I know a woman in Pennsylvania with two little children. The woman calls you husband and those children call you father and they are hunting everywhere for you and they can't find you. They don't know where you are. Right over there is another woman with six children hanging to her skirts and she calls you husband and they call you father. Brother, you have no business in that desk.'

"The preacher made one lunge for the tent flap and vanished. His brother, who was sitting in the audience, sprang to his feet, telling the stunned audience, 'Brethren, the worst of it is, it is all true.' "

"Elder Armitage told this story in the Redlands, California, church in early 1931, where G. B. Starr was pastor." But there is more. "When Elder Armitage told it in Redlands he also said that when his mother died, his father married the sister of that Wisconsin woman with the six children. All of the six children were church members, one of them 'occupying a very important place in the Loma Linda Sanitarium.' " And they were now his cousins.

Then, Elder Armitage made the story even more dramatic. "He pointed to the mother who had been deceived by her bigamist husband, [who was now his aunt]—she was in the church that day visiting her daughter, one of her six children."

Chapter 12

A Letter in the Nick of Time—Saving Elder Cornell

lder Merritt E. Cornell was born in 1827, the same year as Ellen White. He was led to the Seventh-day Adventist Church by Joseph Bates in 1852 and immediately set out vigorously to proclaim his new faith. He and Elder Loughborough conducted the first Adventist tent meetings in Battle Creek in 1854, one year before the church leaders moved the publishing house and their homes from Rochester, New York, to Battle Creek. He and Loughborough surely led the way.

In June 1871, then forty-four years old, Cornell joined Loughborough in evangelistic meetings conducted in San Francisco, California. More than fifty were baptized and a church was organized. Cornell's wife, Angeline, had been working with him as the first Seventh-day Adventist Bible instructor, sometimes remaining behind to teach new converts the essentials of the Adventist message. And perhaps that set up an incident in San Francisco that probably saved his marriage.

However, as the meetings progressed, Cornell grew careless in his conduct, especially with female companions. Loughborough, with the gentleness of Paul, admonished Cornell to shun every appearance of evil. Much to Loughborough's surprise, Cornell took a bold and defiant attitude, declaring that he had a right to do as he pleased.

Loughborough went back to Sonoma County to oversee about five churches that he had organized with D. T. Bourdeau. When Loughborough returned to San Francisco, he saw immediately that the church was buzzing. Cornell had friends who strongly sympathized with him, but a larger group saw the pending crisis. The situation worsened rapidly. Cornell was a moth about to be consumed by the flame. Many before him and since could not resist the fatal attraction.

On Sabbath, January 27, 1872, the church decided that an investigation was needed. Something decisive had to be done to save the reputation of the young church. The time was set for the next morning, Sunday, January 28, at nine o'clock.

Sunday morning, when Loughborough was walking to the meeting, he met Cornell weeping and stating that he was not going to the meeting. Loughborough replied, "Not going to the meeting? The meeting relates to your case!"

"I know that," said Cornell, "but I am all wrong. You are right in the position you have taken in reference to me. Here is a letter of confession I have written to the church; you take it and read it to them. It will be better for you, and better for those who might be inclined to sympathize with me, if I am not there."

Loughborough, much surprised, asked, "What has occasioned this great change in you since yesterday?"

Cornell replied, " 'I went to the post office last night, after the Sabbath, and received a letter from Sister White, from Battle Creek, Michigan. It is a testimony she has written out for me.' Handing it to me, he said, 'Read that, and you will see how the Lord sees my case.' "

Here was Ellen White's message:

Battle Creek, Michigan, December 27, 1871. Dear Brother Cornell, You will see before this reaches you that the Lord has again visited His people by giving me a testimony. In this view I was shown that you were not standing in the clear light and you are in danger of bringing a reproach upon the cause of God by moving as you happen to feel. It is Satan's intent to destroy you. . . .

I was shown that you now should be very circumspect in your deportment and in your words. You are watched by enemies. You have great weaknesses for a man that is as strong as you are to move the crowd. . . . If you are not cautious, you will bring a reproach upon the cause of God which could not soon be wiped away.[1]

"Cornell requested Loughborough to say to the church that he had received a testimony from Sister White, reproving him for his conduct, and that he accepted it, as it was the truth. The church was saved from division. It was clear to all that there was divine timing in this unique experience. Loughborough did some checking, and wrote:

> This was part of a view given to Mrs. White at Bordoville, Vermont, December 10, 1871. She began to write the part relating to this brother's case December 27, 1871, but for some reason the completion of the document was delayed until January 18, 1872, at which time it was finished and mailed from Battle Creek. It then required about nine days to get letters overland from Michigan to California. . . .
>
> At the time of the vision [in early December] there was but a shadow of what was actually developed when the testimony arrived in San Francisco. It will be seen, from a comparison of dates, that the culmination of the case in San Francisco came after the written testimony left the former place. Our brethren in San Francisco saw at once that no person could have written to Battle Creek and communicated the intelligence to Mrs. White in time for her to write this letter, for the state of things did not then exist.

"Loughborough . . . was naturally curious as to the exact timing of the message. This is what his investigation uncovered:

> At a very early hour on the morning of January 18, 1872, Mrs. White was awakened with the above testimony vividly impressed upon her mind. The impression was as distinct to her as though audibly spoken, 'Write out immediately that

testimony for California, and get it into the very next mail; it is needed.' This being repeated the second time, she arose, hastily dressed, and completed the writing.

Just before breakfast she handed it to her son Willie, saying, 'Take this letter to the post office, but don't put it into the drop. Hand it to the postmaster, and have him be sure to put it into the mailbag that goes out this morning.'

He afterward said that he thought her instructions a little peculiar, but he asked no questions, and did as he was bidden and 'saw the letter go into the mailbag.' "

What have we learned? Had Ellen White written out the vision in December 1871 and mailed it as was her custom, the message would have had little application. Had the letter come on the following Monday, the day after the Sunday church meeting, the church would have been torn apart and left with bitter feelings. That letter reached Elder Cornell at precisely the right time.

Elder Cornell accepted the rebuke, ceased his inappropriate behavior, and continued his evangelistic ministry with Elder Loughborough.

A few years later, Ellen White wrote: "I have been aroused from my sleep with a vivid sense of subjects previously presented to my mind; and I have written, at midnight, letters that have gone across the continent and, arriving at a crisis, have saved great disaster to the cause of God. This has been my work for many years."[2]

[1]Letter 23, 1871.
[2]*Testimonies,* vol. 5, 671.

Chapter 13

The Phantom Ship—
Dudley Canright

D udley M. Canright was a forceful, articulate speaker and writer who had much ability to offer the Adventist Church. James White recognized Canright's potential when, at age twenty-one, Canright asked for counsel regarding his future. White spent about an hour encouraging him. He also gave Canright a Bible and a pair of charts, saying, "Here Dudley, take these, go out and try it. When you become satisfied that you have made a mistake, bring them back."

The next May, White met Canright and asked, "What about those charts and the Bible?" And Canright replied, "Brother White, you have lost them." In 1865, when he was twenty-six, Canright was ordained. He first worked with leading evangelists and later made his own way throughout the Midwest and some eastern states. Canright was soon a conference president and served on the General Conference committee for two years.

But some years later, Canright's emotions outran his judgment, and he chafed under both administrative control and the close guidance of Ellen White. Dudley Canright was a man of much ability but was plagued with recurring periods of doubts and discouragements. In the fall of 1882, he gave up preaching and went to farming in Otsego, Michigan.

By September 1884—two years later—at the camp meeting in Jackson, Michigan, Canright publicly confessed his error in giving up preaching and stated that now his doubts had vanished. He returned to preaching as a changed man. The October 7, 1884, *Review and Herald* carried an article in which Canright reviewed his troubles. He referred back eleven years to a testimony from Ellen White that he and his wife had rejected. And to another in 1879 that they rejected. Canright wrote that, after reexamining these experiences, he now saw that he "had put a wrong meaning on some things, and that other things were certainly true. . . . I could truly say that I believed the testimonies. All my hard feelings toward Sister White vanished in a moment, and I felt a tender love toward her. Everything looked different."

In referring to the Jackson camp meeting, he wrote,

I felt in my heart the most remarkable change that I ever experienced in all my life. It was a complete reversion of all my feelings. . . . I want to say to all my friends that now I not only accept but believe the testimonies to be from God. Knowing the opposition I have felt to them, this change in my feelings is more amazing to myself than it can be to others.

I am fully satisfied that my own salvation and my usefulness in saving others depends upon my being connected with this people and this work. And here I take my stand to risk all I am, or have, or hope for, in this life and the life to come, with this people and this work.

During the years that Canright was a faithful Adventist, he also served as a Bible teacher at Battle Creek College and as the author of Sabbath School lessons, two books, and many pamphlets. Ellen White was often in the Canright home and wrote joyfully of her visits.

But by late 1886, old weaknesses reappeared after Canright had been passed over for several administrative positions, including president of the Michigan Conference.

His closest friend, George I. Butler, wrote in the church paper, December 1887, regarding Canright's latest and last defection in February 1887: "When everything went pleasantly, he could usually see things with clearness. When he was *abused,* as he always thought he was when things did not go to suit him, the evidences of our faith began immediately to grow dim."

These events were the background for a letter Ellen White wrote to Canright from Basel, Switzerland:

> Dear Brother M [Canright]: I had an impressive dream last night. I thought that you were on a strong vessel, sailing on very rough waters. Sometimes the waves beat over the top, and you were drenched with water. You said: "I shall get off; this vessel is going down." "No," said one who appeared to be the captain, "this vessel sails into the harbor. She will never go down." But you answered: "I shall be washed overboard. As I am neither captain nor mate, who cares? I shall take my chances on that vessel you see yonder." Said the captain: "I shall not let you go there, for I know that vessel will strike the rocks before she reaches the harbor." You straightened yourself up, and said with great positiveness: "This vessel will become a wreck; I can see it just as plain as can be." The captain looked upon you with piercing eye, and said firmly: "I shall not permit you to lose your life by taking that boat. The timbers of her framework are worm-eaten, and she is a deceptive craft. If you had more knowledge you could discern between the spurious and the genuine, the holy and that appointed to utter ruin."
>
> I awoke, but it is this dream that leads me to write to you. I was feeling deeply over some of these things when a letter came, saying that you were "under great temptation and trial." What is it, Brother M? Is Satan tempting you again? Is God permitting you to be brought to the same place where you have failed before? Will you now let unbelief take possession of your soul? Will you fail every time, as did the children of Israel? God help you to resist the devil and to come forth stronger from every trial of your faith!
>
> Be careful how you move. Make straight paths for your feet. Close the door to unbelief and make God your strength. If perplexed, hold still; make no move in the dark. I am deeply concerned for your soul. This may be the last trial that God will grant you. Advance not one step in the downward road to

perdition. Wait, and God will help you. Be patient, and the clear light will appear. If you yield to impressions you will lose your soul, and the soul is of great value with God.[1]

Sadly, Canright did not heed the warning in this letter. What became of Canright, who at that time was still in his forties? For a few years, he preached for Baptist churches but never was featured in their assemblies. His congregations dwindled, and eventually he spent his time writing books attacking Seventh-day Adventists and selling books for children. His 1889 book, *Seventh-Day Adventism Renounced,* has been analyzed and refuted in W. H. Branson's *In Defense of the Faith* (1933), as well as by other authors.

In his later years, Canright was remembered as a "tall, poorly clad, elderly gentleman" who would come to the Battle Creek Sanitarium kitchen through the kitchen's back door with his "courtesy meal ticket" and eat at the workers' table. "He stood straight, and his bearing indicated that he had been a man of some distinction. . . . His uncut hair, his untrimmed and dirty fingernails, his unkempt attire, the absence of one eye, made this stranger somewhat repulsive to the girls who waited on him." They called him, "Mr. X." until they were better informed.

On July 24, 1915, Dudley M. Canright attended Ellen White's funeral service at Battle Creek. Ellen had predicted Canright's perilous journey and wept when he chose to enter the phantom ship of another denomination. Eyewitnesses described the touching, uncontrollable grief of Canright in his last parting from Mrs. White. After the long line of mourners had passed the casket, Canright suggested to his brother, Jasper, that he would like one more, last farewell. Jasper wrote later, "My brother rested his hand on the side of the casket, and with tears falling down his cheeks, he said brokenly, "There's a noble Christian woman gone."

---

[1] *Testimonies,* vol. 5, 571.

Chapter 14

Secret Masonic Signs— N. D. Faulkhead

ecember 1892, and the first term of the Australasian Bible School had just ended, much to the delight of Ellen White. She had invested personal funds to get the school started, had asked for loans from friends, and had given much personal support for the new leaders. She was now sixty-five years old.

The closing ceremonies were over, but Ellen White had more work to do before the day ended. Willie White had called a meeting of the school board to make plans for the next school year. The treasurer of the publishing house, N. D. Faulkhead, was in his office when Willie told him that Ellen White wanted to see him before he left the campus. As he walked down the hallway toward her room, Faulkhead remembered a dream he had had several nights before in which Ellen White had a message for him.

"Mr. Faulkhead was a tall, keen, apt, and energetic businessman. When he became a Seventh-day Adventist, he held membership in several secret organizations, but he did not withdraw from these. As he wrote of his experience some years later in a general letter to 'My Dear Brethren in the Faith,' he told of these affiliations:

I was closely connected with the Masonic Lodge, . . . I held the highest positions in the following lodges that could be conferred upon me: first, I was Master of the Master Masons' Lodge (or Blue Lodge); second, I was First Principal of the Holy Royal (of Canada); third, I was Preceptor of the Knights Templars, besides many other minor lodges, the Good Templars, Rechabites, and Odd Fellows, in which I also held high positions."

When the Faulkhead family became Adventists, "his unusual ability was recognized, and he was employed as treasurer in the Echo Publishing Company. He served well at first, but as time advanced he became more and more engrossed in his lodge work, and his interests in the work of God began to wane.

"This was his situation when Ellen White arrived in Australia in December, 1891. . . . A few days after her arrival," she had a vision that opened up to her matters involving the publishing house in general; she "penned testimonies to a number of the individuals involved, including Mr. Faulkhead and his wife. The document addressed to them dealt with his connection with the publishing house and his affiliation with the Masonic Lodge, and filled fifty pages. When she thought to mail it to him, she was restrained from doing so. She said, 'When I enclosed the communication all ready to mail, it seemed that a voice spoke to me saying, "Not yet, not yet, they will not receive your testimony." ' "

Ellen White kept that document for almost twelve months, all the while maintaining "a deep interest in Mr. and Mrs. Faulkhead and their spiritual welfare. Some of his associates in the publishing house were very much concerned as they observed his growing infatuation with the work of the lodge and his" decreasing interest in the publishing house. "They pleaded with him, urging him to consider the danger of his course. 'But,' as Mr. Faulkhead states 'my heart was full of those things; in fact, I thought more of them than I did of anything else.'

"He defiantly met the appeals with the bold statement 'that he would not give up his connection with the Freemasons for all that [Elder] Starr or White or any other minister might say. He knew what he was about, and he was not going to be taught by them.' It was clear to those in charge of the work that unless a marked change came in his attitude, he would soon have to find other employment."

In early December, a few days before the school board meeting, "J. H. Stockton, one of the first Seventh-day Adventists in Australia, was talking with Mr. Faulkhead. He asked him what he would do if

Ellen White had a testimony for him in regard to his connection with the lodge. To this Faulkhead boldly replied: 'It would have to be mighty strong.' Neither man was aware that almost a year before, the entire matter had been opened to her."

A few days later, "on Saturday night, December 10, . . . Mr. Faulkhead dreamed that the Lord had shown his case to Ellen White, and that she had a message for him." Now, three days later, "Faulkhead found Ellen White, who greeted him cordially. He asked her whether she had something for him. She replied that the burden of his case was upon her mind, and that she had a message for him from the Lord, which she wished him and his wife to hear. She called for a meeting in the near future, when she would present that message. Faulkhead eagerly asked, 'Why not give me the message now?' "

Ellen White picked up the manuscript. "She told Faulkhead that several times she had prepared to send the message, but that she 'had felt forbidden by the Spirit of the Lord to do so.'. . .

"She then read and talked. A part of the fifty pages that were read that evening was of a general nature, relating to the work in the Echo Publishing Company. . . . But the major part dealt specifically with Mr. Faulkhead's experience and his connection not only with the work of the office but also his affiliation with the Masonic Lodge. She read to him of his efforts to maintain high principles for which the lodge claimed to stand, often couching her message in Masonic language. She also told him where in the lodge hall she had seen him sitting. . . . She spoke of his increasing interest in the work of these organizations and of his waning interest in the cause of God; of her seeing in vision his dropping the small coins from his purse in the Sabbath offering plate and the larger coins into the coffers of the lodge. She heard him addressed as 'Worshipful Master.' "

Faulkhead later wrote: "I thought this was getting pretty close home when she started to talk to me in reference to what I was doing in the lodges."

But Ellen was not finished. She earnestly warned that " 'unless he severed every tie that bound him to these associations, he would lose his soul.' Then, giving a certain movement with her hand that was made by her guide, she said, 'I cannot relate all that was given to me.'

"At this, Faulkhead turned pale. Recounting the incident, he wrote:

> Immediately she gave me this sign. I touched her on the shoulder and asked her if she knew what she had done. She looked up surprised and said she did not do anything unusual. I told her that she had given me the sign of a Knight Templar. Well, she did not know anything about it.

"They talked on. She spoke further of Freemasonry and the impossibility of a man being a Freemason and a wholehearted Christian. Again she made a certain movement, which," she wrote later, " 'my attending angel made to me.'

"Again Mr. Faulkhead started, and the blood left his face. A second time she had made a secret sign, one known only to the highest order of Masons. It was a sign that no woman could know, for it was held in the strictest secrecy—the place of meeting was guarded both inside and outside against strangers. 'This convinced me that her testimony was from God,' he stated.

"Speaking further of his reaction to this, he wrote:

> I can assure you . . . this caused me to feel very queer. But, as Sister White said, the Spirit of the Lord had come upon me and taken hold of me. She went on talking and reading as if nothing had happened, but I noticed how her face brightened up when I interrupted her again and spoke to her about the sign. She seemed surprised that she had given me such a sign. She did not know that she had moved her hand. Immediately the statement that I had made to Brother Stockton, that it would have to be mighty strong before I could believe that she had a message for me from the Lord, flashed through my mind.

"When Mrs. White finished reading, tears were in the man's eyes. He said:

> I accept every word. All of it belongs to me. . . . I accept the light the Lord has sent me through you. I will act upon it. I

am a member of five lodges, and three other lodges are under my control. I transact all of their business. Now I shall attend no more of their meetings, and shall close my business relations with them as fast as possible.

"He also stated: 'I am so glad you did not send me that testimony, for then it would not have helped me.'"

The written testimony without the secret hand signals would not have convinced Faulkhead that Ellen White was indeed a messenger of the Lord.

"When Mr. Faulkhead left Ellen White's room, the hour was late. He took the streetcar to the railway station, and while traveling up Collins Street, he passed the lodge hall. It suddenly dawned upon him that he should have been there attending a Knights Templar meeting that very evening. As he neared the station, he saw the train for Preston pulling out, so he was obliged to walk the rest of the way home. He chose an unfrequented road so that he might have opportunity for meditation. . . . He so much wanted to meet Daniells, Starr, or W. C. White and tell them that he was a new man, and how free and how happy he felt in his decision to sever his connection with all secret societies. It seemed to him that a ton of weight had rolled from his shoulders. And to think that the God who rules the universe and guides the planets had seen his danger and sent a message just for him!"

The next morning Mr. Faulkhead told his co-workers what had happened the night before. He then "called in his assistant and dictated his resignation to the various lodges. Then A. G. Daniells came in, and Mr. Faulkhead told him of his experience. While the two were talking, his letters of resignation were passed to Mr. Faulkhead for his signature. He signed and enclosed them and handed them to Daniells to mail. . . .

"But no sooner had Faulkhead given the letters to Daniells than a feeling of mistrust came over him; he felt that he should have mailed the letters himself. Then he thanked the Lord for what he had done, for he felt that he could not have trusted himself to mail the letters.

"On Thursday, December 15, Mr. Faulkhead, accompanied by his wife, had another interview with Mrs. White. A number of pages of new matter were read to the two of them, and it was all accepted. 'I wish you to know,' he told Mrs. White, 'how I look upon this matter. I regard myself as greatly honored of the Lord. He has seen fit to mention me, and I am not discouraged, but encouraged. I shall follow out the light given me of the Lord.' "

But the battle was not over. Faulkhead's "lodge friends refused to release him, so he had to serve out his terms of office, another nine months. Most determined efforts were put forth to hold him to their society, but he had taken a firm position and stood by it. At times his church associates trembled for him. Ellen White wrote encouraging letters in support of his stand. He was victorious at last.

"With the expiration of his term as officer of several of the lodges, the complete victory was won, and Mr. Faulkhead was able, on September 18, 1893, to write to Ellen White and her son.

Dear Brother and Sister White:

It gives me much pleasure to tell you that my term of office as Master of the Masonic Lodge expired last month. And I feel to thank God for it. How thankful I am to Him for sending me a warning that I was traveling on the wrong road. I do praise Him for His goodness and His love shown toward me, in calling me from among that people. I can see now very clearly that to continue with them would have been my downfall, as I must confess that my interest for the truth was growing cold. But thanks be to God, He did not let me go on with them without giving me warning through His servant. I cannot express my gratitude to Him for it. . . .

I can praise God with all my might, and then I cannot express my gratitude to Him for the love that He has shown me.

N. D. Faulkhead

"This experience brought great confidence to . . . church members in Australia, and it was ever a source of encouragement . . . to Mr. Faulkhead. With the renewal of his first love and interest in the cause of God, he continued to serve the publishing house for many years, giving his time and strength and life to the spreading of the message."

Chapter 15

Why, on My Platform?— Nathaniel Davis

*A*t times I am carried far ahead into the future and shown what is to take place. Then again I am shown things as they have occurred in the past. After I come out of vision I do not at once remember all that I have seen, and the matter is not so clear before me until I write, then the scene rises before me as was presented in vision, and I can write with freedom. Sometimes the things which I have seen are hid from me after I come out of vision, and I cannot call them to mind until I am brought before a company where that vision applies, then the things which I have seen come to my mind with force. I am just as dependent upon the Spirit of the Lord in relating or writing a vision, as in having the vision. It is impossible for me to call up things which have been shown me unless the Lord brings them before me at the time that He is pleased to have me relate or write them.[1]

The story of Nathaniel Davis is one example of perhaps hundreds that bear out the truth of this statement Ellen White penned in 1860. Ellen wrote much about the drama of the great controversy, expanding on how God and Satan were working out their sides in the conflict. Frequently Ellen White's insights made the difference when great issues arose in the world work of the Seventh-day Adventist Church. But often she focused upon the struggles of lonely men and women, one by one, who needed light and hope and salvation in their conflict with evil.

Nattie, as his friends called him, became a Seventh-day Adventist some time around 1895, about midway in Ellen White's time in Australia. A friend described him as a lanky man of "about six feet five inches." Ellen White characterized him as a man with "advantages in education . . . pleasing abilities," with "clear insight into [God's] Word," and "blessed . . . with powers to communicate that Word in an acceptable manner."[2]

Ellen's first connection with Nattie came when he wrote her an eight-page letter on September 9, 1896. She was sixty-nine. It is an amazingly troubled letter. He described himself as having "dishonored my Lord, disgraced my profession, made shipwreck of faith, and am now in despair, for I see only the blankest ruin, and . . . I have no one to blame but myself." He closed his letter, "Yours in fear and trembling."

Nattie had admitted his problems were prompted by "personal enmities, greed, and envy." He had lost his position as colporteur and could not find secular employment because of the Sabbath. He was also in great debt to the publishing house. His wife did not yet know about his job loss and debt, but he feared she would discover how things really were.

But Nattie had even bigger problems. In August of the following year, 1897, Nattie visited with Ellen in Sydney. In her diary she wrote:

> I had a long conversation with Brother Davis this morning. Poor man, he is in trouble. He once dabbled with spiritualism and theosophy, and its dark influence has shrouded him ever since. Although he sees the truth and believes the truth, yet there seems to be a bondage to this power that is hard for him to break. I could only bid him "Look and live." An uplifted Saviour will heal the serpent's bite, and although its poison has been diffused through his entire being, I could say to him, "Look and live.". . . May the Lord deliver him from the cruel power of Satan is my prayer.[3]

But Nattie was persistent. A few days later, August 15, Nattie again met with Ellen at her home in Cooranbong. During the night she had a clear picture of his problem, and she began a letter not finished until several days later.

The substance of that letter was (1) *Nattie was under the control of satanic agencies.* She wrote: "If you determine to break the power of satanic agencies that is upon you, present your case before the servants of God, humble your heart before God, and ask them to pray for you that God will have mercy upon you."[4]

(2) *Nattie was deeply in debt.* Ellen White, generous as she always was, stated that she was about to enclose some money in the letter, but the Holy Spirit immediately prohibited her impulse to help: "The Spirit of the Lord teaches me that as you now are this would be using the Lord's money to hurt yourself and other souls." And she gave him some practical advice as to how to dig out from under his huge burden.

(3) *Nattie was chained to immorality.* She wrote: "You have vile thoughts, and have corrupted your ways before God. . . . Your course is immoral. You are bringing disgrace upon the cause of truth. . . . You have brought moral corruption upon souls. You are a dangerous man to be left to yourself anywhere." Ellen White pleaded with Nattie as she would her own son to mend his ways, but he had not heeded her advice.

It is easy to guess why Nattie did not want to appeal to church leaders for their help—he had secret sins that he did not want to share, even with his wife. Besides, he was now employed in the publishing office.

Later that summer of 1897, an event happened on a Sabbath afternoon in North Fitzroy, a suburb of Melbourne, that opened the eyes of Harold Blunden, a young teenager who later became the publishing director for the General Conference. I knew him well during his retirement in northern California.

Perhaps like many other Australians, the concept of an "American lady prophet" troubled Harold Blunden. As he said later, "Surely there were enough *Australians* around, that God need not pick an *American!* And surely there were enough *men* available, that God need not choose a *woman!* "

Mrs. White was to speak in his little red brick chapel on Sabbath afternoon. Herold went early and took a seat on the aisle in the second row from the front. He wanted to see and hear everything. The chapel eventually filled, leaving standing room only.

When Mrs. White's train was delayed nearly two hours, the audience spent the time singing and giving personal testimonies.

Finally Ellen appeared, walking on the arm of the young American missionary, Arthur Daniells, president of the recently organized Australasian Union Conference. After introducing Ellen, Pastor Daniells took one of the two empty seats on the rostrum among the other ministers.

Ellen carried a sheaf of manuscripts in her hand that she laid on the pulpit. Looking up at the audience, she smiled and opened her mouth to speak—but nothing came out. She seemed surprised and scanned the audience.

Then she adjusted her manuscript again and opened her mouth—and again no words. She again surveyed the audience, more slowly this time. Then she turned around to look at the faces of those seated on the rostrum.

With her back to the audience, what she next said could be heard only by those in the first few rows. Noticing Nathaniel Davis sitting next to Elder Daniells, she asked the president why Davis was on the same platform with her.

Nattie rose to his full height of six feet five inches, towering above the five-foot two-inch American prophet. He gave her a hateful look and walked off the platform, down the center aisle, and out of the chapel.

Ellen White adjusted her manuscript, smiled, and again opened her mouth—this time speaking for the next hour and a quarter. But young Blunden heard little of the message. He kept asking himself, *What does this all mean?*

As soon as he could after the service, Blunden went to Elder Daniells—and this is what he discovered: Nathaniel Davis had problems with money, women, and spiritualism. Sitting on the platform that Sabbath afternoon, he was a living representative of satanic darkness. God would not loosen the prophet's mouth until this darkness departed.

Teenager Blunden had wanted to test the prophet, but he never expected this kind of test! For young Blunden, the issue was settled. He said, "I never had any problems or questions about Ellen White after that. . . . I know, I was there. I was an eyewitness."

What about Nathaniel Davis? Because Nattie would not or could not initiate further contact with church leaders, Mrs. White urged Daniells and others to help Davis break with the evil spirits that possessed him. On September 2, she followed up with a letter to Davis that she asked Daniells to read to him.

This is how Daniells reported the experience:

> When I began reading it to him, he became very much excited. After a little, I heard some sort of disturbance, and looking up, saw him with an open knife in his raised hand. I asked, "What is the matter?" He grated his teeth and glared at me like a madman.
>
> His wife and I appealed to him to put the knife down, but he was menacing us so wildly that I did not dare to go on reading. I did not know whether he would thrust it into me or his wife or himself. I said, "Let us kneel down and pray to God. There is a God in Israel who can help us, and we must have His help."
>
> We knelt down, and I may tell you that I was never in a more perplexing place. I knew that demons were in the room and I knew that we must have the power of that same Christ who subdued demons and cast out devils while among men.
>
> The first thing I said was "O Lord, we come to Thee in the all-prevailing name of Jesus." At the mention of the name Jesus, that man hurled his knife across the room with terrible violence. At the mention of the all-powerful name of Jesus he broke into sobs and the violence disappeared. After his wife and I had prayed, he prayed most earnestly to God to deliver him from those tormenting devils.

After they arose, Nattie said, "Brother Daniells, every word of it is true. For weeks I have been tormented by these evil spirits. I have been thrown out of my bed, and I have been hammered on the floor by those demons; it has wrecked my nerves, and I was about to give up to them and become their obedient slave again."[5]

Three years later, on August 29, 1900, Ellen White left Sydney harbor on the *Moana*, sailing for San Francisco. Before she left, her friends handed her an attractive autograph album. In it they had written daily messages for her to read, a message for each day. Exactly seven days into the voyage, on September 4, Ellen White opened the album for that day's greeting. It had been penned on August 6 and was signed "N. A. Davis."

It affords me the most sincere pleasure to have the privilege of putting on record my appreciation of Sister E. G. White's work and my gratitude to my heavenly Father for the messages sent through her to His people.

The faithful witness, thus bourne, revealed to me the means whereby the bondage of Satan was broken when, owing to the influence of spiritualism, I had well nigh become a spiritual wreck.

I have every reason to be positive in my confidence in Sister E. G. White as a true prophet.

May the Lord of love and mercy, grace and truth, guide and guard her safely to the end, and lengthen her days so that she may continue to warn, admonish, and strengthen the remnant people of God.

Who told Ellen White about Nattie? Certainly no one in Australia. Who closed her mouth when she tried to speak that Sabbath afternoon?

This autograph album now rests in the White Estate office in Silver Spring, Maryland, for those who may want to read Nattie's parting words for themselves. God, and His prophets, do care about people, one by one. "Believe in the LORD your God, so shall ye be established; believe his prophets, so shall ye prosper" (2 Chronicles 20:20).

---

[1]*Spiritual Gifts* (1860), vol. 2, 292, 293. *Selected Messages*, bk. 1, 36.
[2]Letter 36, 1897.
[3]*Manuscript Releases*, vol. 13, 3, 4.
[4]Letter 36, 1897.
[5]*Australasian Record*, August 13, 1928.

Chapter 16

Voting on the Sabbath— Des Moines, Iowa

*I*n the summer of 1881, both James and Ellen White were ill. She was fifty-three, and James, fifty-nine. James, the tired warrior, would be dead in a few weeks.

Nevertheless, James and Ellen did their usual part at the early June camp meeting at Spring Arbor, Michigan. After the Michigan camp meeting was over, Ellen had the deep impression, "Go to Iowa; I have a work for you to do." The Iowa meeting would begin in only a few days—but was many miles away. Ellen wrote in a letter that she regarded the trip to Iowa as difficult as if she had to go to Europe. When she told her weary husband, James, about the impression, he responded, "We will go."

When they arrived in Des Moines, she said to a minister, "Well, we are here at the Lord's bidding, for what special purpose we do not know, but we shall doubtless know as the meeting progresses."

The Whites, as usual, did much of the preaching. On Sunday evening, after Ellen had retired to her tent for the night, the conference constituency conducted a business meeting on the subject of voting, especially in regard to temperance and prohibition. Later that evening, the message came to Ellen that the group wanted her counsel.

Elder G. B. Starr recalled later that Ellen White had related a dream that evening describing the Iowa circumstance although not knowing just how and where it applied. The heavenly spokesman had said: "God designs to help the people in a great movement on this subject. He also designed that you, as a people, should be the head and not the tail in the movement; but now the position you have taken will place you at the tail."

In the meeting, Mrs. White was asked whether the Iowa Adventists should vote for prohibition. Her answer was swift: "Yes, to a man, everywhere, and perhaps I shall shock some of you if I say, If necessary, vote on the Sabbath for prohibition if you cannot at any other time."

Writing later, Starr emphasized: "I can testify that the effect of the relating of that dream was electrical upon the whole conference. A convincing power attended it, and I saw for the first time the unifying power of the gift of prophecy in the church."

It would take a large book indeed to track the travels of Ellen White and the profound effect she had on decisions that were being made. The historian today would have an impossible task if he or she attempted to separate Ellen White and her influence from the history of the Seventh-day Adventist Church.

Chapter 17

"Last Night! Last Night!"— Salamanca Vision and Battle Creek

One of the most interesting, most convincing of Ellen White's two thousand visions is known as the Salamanca vision. The occasion: the March 1891 General Conference session in Battle Creek, Michigan. The presence of Ellen White kept denominational leaders from making serious mistakes in decisions about the church's religious liberty program and publishing policies.

A portion of the remarkable events surrounding this vision began in November 1890, several months before the General Conference session was to be held in Michigan. Salamanca, a small town in western New York State near the Pennsylvania line, has been famous among Adventist circles ever since because of a remarkable vision Ellen White received there.

As was her custom, Ellen began to write out the vision in her diary-journal. But she didn't write out the entire vision at once. Sometimes she left blank pages or half pages, knowing that she could fill them in later as God continued to fill in the details. But when she tried to write or tell in public a particularly dramatic scene she had viewed in the Salamanca vision, Ellen's mind repeatedly went blank. Consequently, those pages remained blank, month after month.

Ellen had many opportunities to apply much of the vision's message to current conditions in the church, but the central feature of the vision was withheld from her memory. Looking back, we can now see that if Ellen had reported the entire vision at any time other than one particular weekend at the March General Conference, she would have been considered an outright fraud.

At that March General Conference, one of the issues was the pending danger of muting distinctive Adventist beliefs, especially in denominational periodicals. Leaders in the Religious Liberty Department believed that Adventists would have greater recognition in their periodical, the *American Sentinel,* if they dropped the term *Seventh-day Adventist* from its columns and said nothing about the seventh-day Sabbath. Ellen had said on several occasions that this policy was "the first step in a succession of wrong steps."

In her Sabbath-afternoon sermon at the General Conference session, Ellen emphasized again the peril of such thinking. Uriah Smith, the editor of the church paper, summarized her sermon:

> Sister White spoke on the importance of preaching the Word, and the danger of covering up, and keeping in the background, the distinctive features of our faith, under the impression that prejudice will thereby be avoided. If there is committed to us a special message, as we believe, that message must go, without reference to the customs or prejudices of the world, not governed by a policy of fear or favor. Some will receive and be sanctified through it, though multitudes will oppose and reject it. . . .
>
> The discourse was a timely one, and made a profound impression upon the large congregation.

A. T. Robinson observed something else regarding that afternoon sermon: "Three times she attempted to tell the scene that passed before her at the Salamanca meeting; each time her mind would seem to turn in another channel. At the third reference to the Salamanca meeting, she remarked, in an almost impatient tone of voice, 'But I will have more to say about that some other time.'"

After the meeting, the president of the General Conference, Elder Olsen, asked Ellen if she would speak at the early morning ministers' meeting on Sunday. She replied that she had already done her part and was weary, so other plans were made. Ellen told her secretarial workers that they could sleep in Sunday morning, and so would she. They were ecstatic—a morning to sleep in and not work as usual.

While walking to the five-thirty meeting the next morning, Ellen's son Willie and two others passed Ellen's home and noticed that the lights were on. Willie said that he would stop in to see whether his mother was ill. He found her busily writing, a task she had been doing for two hours. Ellen reported that God had awakened her about three o'clock and told her to go to the ministers' meeting and relate some things shown her at Salamanca.

So off Ellen went with the three men. When they arrived, the meeting had already begun. Elder Olsen recalled that Ellen "walked in with a bundle of manuscript under her arm." At the close of the prayer, Ellen "arose and stated that she had not expected to attend this meeting" but that "she was impressed that she should present some things that had been shown her in November the year before . . . at Salamanca."

Ellen reviewed the many times she had tried to reveal portions of that vision. But now she added something more. She described how her Guide said, "Follow Me" and led her into a council of men where she said much zeal and earnestness were manifested, but not much knowledge. One in the group held up the *Sentinel* (the religious liberty journal) and with his hand across the paper said, " 'This must come out,' and then made remarks entirely contrary to the principles of our faith."

When Ellen had finished speaking, the editor of the magazine, A. F. Ballenger, arose and said with tears, "I was in that council meeting which was held last night until a late hour, and Sister White has described it accurately. The very words she says she heard spoken were spoken last night. I was on the wrong side of the question, and now take my position on the right side."

One who described the meeting said, "I shall never forget the look of perplexity on the face of the dear woman, as she looked at Brother Ballenger and exclaimed, 'Last night! Last night!' "

Captain Eldridge, a key leader at the publishing house spoke:

I was in that meeting. Last night, after the close of the conference, some of us met in my room in the Review office, where we locked ourselves in, and there took up and discussed the questions and the matter that has been presented to us this morning. . . .

If I should have begun to give a description of what took place, and the personal attitude of those in the room, I could not have given it as exactly and correctly as it has been given by Sister White. I now see that I was in error; that the position that I took was not correct; and from the light that has been given this morning, I acknowledge that I was wrong.

Others who attended that late Saturday night and early Sunday morning meeting gave similar testimonies. But one man sat mystified. Elder Olsen, president of the General Conference, wrote of his surprise:

Personally, I sat there in blank bewilderment. I did not know what she referred to. I had neither heard nor had any knowledge of the things that she presented, nor of such a meeting as she described. Indeed, I was so surprised, and the things she presented as having taken place in that meeting seemed so unreasonable, that I was quite nonplused in my mind as to what this meant. She spoke at considerable length, and placed the matter very definitely before us, and showed up the wrong spirit that was manifested, and the erroneousness of the position that had been taken by certain ones in their discussion. . . .

Sister White had had no opportunity to have any knowledge of what had gone on in that room during the night in the Review office. . . . The Lord had shown it to her before the thing took place; and now, the very morning in which it took place, she had been, in a special manner, called by the Lord to present what had been shown her. It is needless to say not only that it brought relief to many minds, but that it gave cause for great thankfulness that at such a critical moment the Lord stepped in and saved us from the perplexity and confusion that seemed to be coming up on important questions.

"The files of the White Estate hold the testimony of others who were present that Sunday morning. One such statement signed by six prominent ministers declares:

> The relation of this vision made a profound and solemn impression upon that large congregation of Seventh-day Adventist ministers present at that early-morning meeting. When they heard those who had been reproved for the wrong course taken in that council confess that all Mrs. White had said about them was true in every particular, they saw the seal of divine inspiration had been set upon that vision and testimony. The power and solemnity of that meeting made an impression upon the minds of those present not soon to be forgotten.

"A. T. Robinson related that those who attended that morning meeting had no breakfast that day:

> The meeting, which began at five-thirty and usually closed at six-thirty, continued until well on in the forenoon. It was one of the most remarkable meetings that it has ever been my privilege to attend. Men of strong iron wills, who the night before manifested a spirit of unyielding stubbornness, confessed with tears and brokenness of voice. Elder Dan Jones said, 'Sister White, I thought I was right. Now I know I was wrong.' "

Everyone clearly understood why Ellen White could not relate this part of the Salamanca vision during the four months she had tried. Especially, it was evident why she was prevented from giving it as she attempted to do three times on Sabbath afternoon in Battle Creek.

Two monumental lessons were learned: (1) the Adventist Church had avoided a serious mistake and (2) all those present had undeniable evidence concerning the reliability and integrity of Ellen White, especially those who held grave doubts during the previous two years that followed the Minneapolis Conference in 1888.

Chapter 18

A Potential Rival— Correcting Two Church Leaders

*I*n 1894 when Ellen White was sixty-seven, another "prophetess" emerged in the Seventh-day Adventist denomination. Her name was Anna Phillips.

This young woman came to believe that God gave her dreams containing advice to other people. Based on those dreams, she wrote "testimonies" to husbands and wives about their personal lives and sent messages to leaders of the church. Many considered Anna to be genuine. A half a world away, while Ellen White was still in Australia, the Holy Spirit, the Spirit of prophecy, made her aware of this development and the harm it was doing to young Anna.

Ellen heard that A. T. Jones, a highly respected minister at that time, was one of those foremost in promoting the "messages" of Anna Phillips. Jones even publicly interspersed Anna's messages with those of Ellen White and then asked the congregation whether they could distinguish between the two authors.

The day following Elder Jones's public endorsement of Anna Phillips in the Battle Creek Church, Jones received a letter from Australia, a letter from Ellen White that had been written many weeks earlier. Jones was so eager to read it that he tore open the envelope in the post office. Part of the letter said, "I have a message for you. Do you suppose that God had commissioned you to take the burden of presenting the visions of Anna Phillips, reading them in public, and uniting them with the testimonies the Lord has been pleased to give me?"

Elder A. O. Tait, a fellow minister, reported that he was with Jones in the post office that day. He noted that tears fell when Elder Jones received this letter the day after his Sabbath sermon. Elder Jones turned to his minister friend and asked: "Who told Sister White a month ago that I was going to preach that sermon about Anna Phillips as a prophetess?"

Elder Tait replied, "Ah, you know, Alonzo."

The following Sabbath at the Battle Creek Church, Elder Jones read portions of Ellen White's letter and apologized to the congregation: "I am wrong, and I confess it. Now I am right." On hearing this letter read, Anna Phillips acknowledged her delusion. She eventually became a faithful, effective Bible instructor. Ellen White had saved the Battle Creek church from discord and a young woman from emotional catastrophe.

But the story is not over. W. W. Prescott, president of Battle Creek College, was also a supporter of Anna Phillips. While visiting Walla Walla College, he planned to introduce the students to Anna Phillips by reading one of her testimonies. Prescott had not been in Battle Creek when Jones had read the letter from Ellen White. Only a few hours before he was scheduled to speak, Prescott received a copy of the same letter from Ellen White.

Elder Stephen Haskell was also visiting Walla Walla at this time, and he reported the events to Ellen White:

> Your testimony came just in season to save some trouble at College Place. I have heard something of the kind before when your letters or testimony would come just at the time when a meeting was in progress and it just reached the people in time to save trouble, but [I] never experienced it before. . . . Brother Prescott was going to read the testimony of Anna Phillips, although we had had some talk over the matter. But the day just in season your letter came and then he of course had opportunity to read it. This settled the question for him. He said, "Then that is all there is to it. Now I will take some of the same medicine that I have given other people." . . . God in His providence had that testimony come on the very train it should have come.

How did Ellen White know when her letter to Prescott and Jones would arrive at the moment when they would be most appreciated? She probably didn't. But the Spirit who guided her did! How did this widespread phenomenon dealing with Anna Phillips work out after the letter to both Jones and Prescott?

Ellen White strongly counseled Battle Creek church members that "Sister Phillips is not to be condemned or denounced. . . . There have been those who have given her wrong impressions; they have flattered and encouraged her, and their words have had an influence upon her life and upon the work she is doing, which she thinks God has given her."

After learning of the confessions of both Jones and Prescott, Ellen wrote a message affirming the men:

> I have more confidence in them today than I have had in the past. . . .
>
> I have the most tender feelings toward our brethren who have made this mistake, and I would say that those who depreciate the ones who have accepted reproof will be permitted to pass through trials which will make manifest their own individual weakness and defects of character. . . .
>
> While I cannot endorse their mistakes, I am in sympathy and union with them in their general work.

In these two anecdotes we see the overarching role of a genuine prophet influencing events thousands of miles away at the most critical moment. But we also see her tenderness to a young woman who had been misled by those she should have been able to trust. Further, we see a prophet in her redeeming, healing mode—always holding out hope for better things to come, if people would heed the counsel from the Lord's messenger.

Chapter 19

Meeting the Iceberg—
Pantheism Crisis, 1903

*E*llen White's challenge "Meet it!" when facing an "iceberg" changed the course of Adventist history in 1903. And her straightforward counsel has been the challenge to church leaders ever since.

Numerous issues crowded the 1903 Autumn Council agenda in Washington, D.C. But one issue loomed above all others—the pantheistic teachings of Dr. John Harvey Kellogg, supported by Dr. E. J. Waggoner, Elder A. T. Jones, and Dr. David Paulson. Dr. Kellogg's book *The Living Temple* seemed to be splitting the leadership of the Adventist Church.

A full day at the Autumn Council was devoted to studying the pantheistic philosophy. All day the delegates wrestled with the matter. "At about nine o'clock in the evening Elder Daniells [president of the General Conference] considered it time to adjourn the meeting, but he did not dare call for a vote. People were too confused and uncertain, and he did not wish to take a step that would solidify any conclusions. So he dismissed the meeting," and the delegates went to their rooms.

Young "Dr. Paulson, who was strongly supportive of Dr. Kellogg, joined Daniells. . . . Reaching the home where Daniells was staying, they stood under a lamppost and chatted for a time. Finally, Dr. Paulson shook his finger at Daniells and declared: 'You are making the mistake of your life. After all this turmoil, some of these days you will wake up to find yourself rolled in the dust, and another will be leading the forces.'

"Elder Daniells straightened up in his weariness . . . and replied firmly: 'I do not believe your prophecy. At any rate, I would rather be rolled in the dust doing what I believe in my soul to be right than to walk with princes, doing what my conscience tells me is wrong.'

"After parting, Daniells entered the home, where he found a group of people awaiting him. They seemed lighthearted and exclaimed, 'Deliverance has come! Here are two messages from Mrs. White.' "

Daniells wrote about this later: "No one can imagine the eagerness with which I read the documents that had come in the mail while we were in the midst of our discussions. There was a most positive testimony regarding the dangerous errors that were taught in *The Living Temple*."

Here is some of the advice he read:

> I have some things to say to our teachers in reference to the new book *The Living Temple*. Be careful how you sustain the sentiments of this book regarding the personality of God. As the Lord presents matters to me, these sentiments do not bear the endorsement of God. They are a snare that the enemy has prepared for these last days. . . .
>
> We need not the mysticism that is in this book.

"The entire manuscript of seven pages . . . may be read in the *Review and Herald* of October 22, 1903." But the story is not over. The second document was addressed to "Leaders in Our Medical Work" and included this counsel:

> After taking your position firmly, wisely, cautiously, make not one concession on any point concerning which God has plainly spoken. Be as calm as a summer evening, but as fixed as the everlasting hills. . . .
>
> In taking this position, I am placed under the necessity of bearing the heavy burden of showing the evil of the plans that I know are not born of heaven. This is the burden

that many times in the past the Lord has laid upon me, in order that His work might be advanced along right lines. How much care and anxiety, how much mental anguish and wearing physical labor, might be saved me in my old age!

But still I am under the necessity of going into the battle, and of discharging in the presence of important assemblies the duty that the Lord has laid upon me—the duty of correcting the wrong course of men who profess to be Christians, but who are doing a work that will have to be undone at a great loss, both financially and in the shaking of the confidence of the people.

"The next morning church leaders assembled for their Council. After the prayer, Elder Daniells arose and told the brethren he had received two important messages from Sister White. . . . They sat in thoughtful silence while he read. As statement after statement setting forth the falsity of the teachings of *The Living Temple* was presented to the assembly, many loud amens were heard and tears flowed freely." At that point the tide was turned against accepting the pantheistic teachings in the book.

Elder Daniells was overwhelmed with these events. A few days later, while the Autumn Council was still in session, he wrote to Ellen White:

We are in the midst of our Council, and I am terribly pressed with work, but I must take a minute this morning to tell you what a wonderful blessing your communications have been to our Council. Never were messages from God more needed than at this very time; and never were messages sent from Him to His people more to the point than those you have sent to us. They have been exactly what we have needed, and have come at just the right time from day to day in our Council. . . . It came at just the right time exactly. The conflict was severe, and we knew not how things would turn. But your clear, clean-cut, beautiful message came and settled the controversy. I do not say that all parties came into perfect harmony, but it gave those who stood on the right side strength to stand, and hold their ground.

A few days later, Daniells referred to a second letter addressed to "The Leaders in Our Medical Work" that he had received from Ellen White.

Your message came on just the right day—a day earlier would have been too soon. I read it to the council yesterday, and it produced a most profound impression. . . .

As for myself, when I received this last communication, I could only sit and weep. For a whole year I had been under a terrible mental strain. I had seen the evil thing, but had not dared to say all that I knew ought to be said. I could not surrender an inch of ground. I knew that it would be wrong to do so, and yet many of my brethren misunderstood me, and charged me with a hard, unyielding spirit, and with a desire to make war. . . .

This communication, calling our brethren to take their stand, brought great relief to me, and the terrible load that had at times almost crushed me, has, in a measure, rolled off from me.

A few days later he wrote to W. C. White, Ellen's son, about the relevance and timeliness of the testimonies he had just received:

It will be impossible for me to find language to state as clearly and forcibly, and I fear, as accurately as I would like the facts relating to the reception, presentation, and influence of the testimonies received from your mother during our recent Council. Never in my life have I seen such signal evidences of the leadership of an all-wise Being as I have seen in connection with the experiences referred to. Only the divine mind could have foreseen our condition and needs, and have sent us the exact help we needed at precisely the right moment. I believe that this is the feeling of nearly every member of the Council.

But there is more to this story, probably the most remarkable part. After "receiving these communications from Elder Daniells, Ellen White wrote to him explaining why he received the messages just when he did:

> Shortly before I sent the testimonies that you said arrived just in time, I had read an incident about a ship in a fog meeting an iceberg. For several nights I slept but little. I seemed to be bowed down as a cart beneath sheaves. One night a scene was clearly presented before me. A vessel was upon the waters, in a heavy fog. Suddenly the lookout cried, 'Iceberg just ahead!' There, towering high above the ship, was a gigantic iceberg. An authoritative voice cried out, 'Meet it!' There was not a moment's hesitation. It was a time for instant action. The engineer put on full steam, and the man at the wheel steered the ship straight into the iceberg. With a crash she struck the ice. There was a fearful shock, and the iceberg broke into many pieces, falling with a noise like thunder upon the deck. The passengers were violently shaken by the force of the collision, but no lives were lost. The vessel was injured, but not beyond repair. She rebounded from the contact, trembling from stem to stern, like a living creature. Then she moved forward on her way.
> Well I knew the meaning of this representation. I had my orders. I had heard the words, like a living voice from our Captain, 'Meet it!' I knew what my duty was, and that there was not a moment to lose. The time for decided action had come. I must without delay obey the command, 'Meet it!'
> This is why you received the testimonies when you did. That night I was up at one o'clock, writing as fast as my hand could pass over the paper.

We have all stood at our posts like faithful sentinels, working early and late to send to the council instruction that we thought would help you.

"Ellen White often began her work at midnight. When her workers came to the office in the morning, they began copying the sheets on which she had written. These were then passed to her for editing. In the meantime she had been writing still more, and all through the day they worked. Then secretaries worked all through the night to get the material ready so that it could be sent on the early-morning train.

"They worked to the last minute, and when they heard the whistle of the train at Barro Station, to the north of Elmshaven, D. E. Robinson, one of the secretaries, jumped on a bicycle with the letters in his pocket. He raced the train almost two miles to the crossing, and then to the station to drop the letters in the mail car. Days later they arrived at their destination just at the hour they were needed. Everyone understood that God's hand was in the work." This episode was just one of many wherein God hovered over His messenger and His message, even down to the very hour and day they were needed, not one day early or one day late.

Chapter 20

Common Sense in Starting School—Elmshaven, January 14, 1904

*E*llen White's common sense was a distinguishing character trait throughout her life. Many chapters could be written about how she exercised common sense in settling arguments on many topics throughout her long ministry.

One of these times occurred in her own living room in Elmshaven on January 14, 1904, when she was seventy-seven. The issue: at what age children should begin schooling. "A church school had been started to serve the Sanitarium church, of which she was a member. . . . Three teachers taught the thirty-five children. . . . However, no provision was made for the younger children, for it was argued Ellen White had counseled . . . that 'parents should be the only teachers of their children until they have reached eight or ten years of age. . . . The only schoolroom for children from eight to ten years of age should be in the open air amid the opening flowers and nature's beautiful scenery. And their only textbook should be the treasures of nature.' "

But a division about the proper age for school enrollment had arisen in the church. So, early on a Thursday morning, the Sanitarium church school board met at Elmshaven in Ellen's living room. Agenda: to "discuss with Ellen White whether the Sanitarium church school should provide schooling for children under the age of ten. . . .

"On a church-wide basis, Seventh-day Adventists were just then beginning to establish schools to accommodate children below the ninth grade. The lower grades had been taught for years at Battle Creek and Healdsburg colleges, but . . . little effort had been made elsewhere."

But the larger issue that morning was how to understand specific Ellen White directives and how church members should relate to them.

In advance of the meeting, Ellen White had learned that children under the age of ten were being denied school privileges because of her earlier statements in the *Testimonies*.

A twenty-five page stenographic report of that important board meeting is on file. Ellen White opened the discussion, saying: "For years, much instruction has been given me in regard to the importance of maintaining firm discipline in the home. I have tried to write out this instruction, and to give it to others."

Ellen then "discussed the responsibilities of parenthood and the importance of right home influences. She dwelt on the responsibility of mothers teaching their children the lessons they should learn in early life." Then she pointed out that, according to the light given to her, many families were far from the ideal:

> Many who enter the marriage relation fail of realizing all the sacred responsibilities that motherhood brings. Many are sadly lacking in disciplinary power. In many homes there is but little discipline, and the children are allowed to do as they please. Such children drift hither and thither; there is nobody in the home capable of guiding them aright, nobody who with wise tact can teach them how to help father and mother, nobody who can properly lay the foundation that should underlie their future education.

Ellen White "was particularly concerned about the influences on the Sanitarium guests of children running loose, 'sharp-eyed, lynx-eyed, wandering about with nothing to do' and 'getting into mischief.'

"Under the circumstances of parental neglect, she declared that according to the light given to her, 'the very best thing that can be done is to have a school,' a 'school for those who can be instructed and have the restraining influence upon them which a school-teacher should exert.'

"She called for a lower department in the Sanitarium school where children as old as 7 or 8 could be instructed. 'They will learn in school that which they frequently do not learn out of school, except by association.' "

Ellen White explained the background of the statement about ten-year-old children she had made years before:

> When I heard what the objections were, that the children could not go to school till they were 10 years old, I wanted to tell you that there was not a Sabbathkeeping school when the light was given to me that the children should not attend school until they were old enough to be instructed. They should be taught at home to know what proper manners were when they went to school, and not be led astray. The wickedness carried on in the common schools is almost beyond conception. That is how it is.

Then "she expressed her concern over what seemed to her an unreasonable application of the *Testimonies*:

> My mind has been greatly stirred in regard to the idea, 'Why, Sister White has said so and so, and Sister White has said so and so; and therefore we are going right up to it.'
>
> God wants us all to have common sense, and He wants us to reason from common sense. Circumstances alter conditions. Circumstances change the relation of things.

"Turning to the board after these opening remarks, she declared: 'I shall not say so much now, because I want to understand just what I should speak on. I want the objections brought forth, why children should not have an education.' "

One teacher pointed out that "if we have any more children, we ought to have some extra help." To this Ellen White responded that many factors should be taken into consideration:

> I want you to take care of what I have said. First, understand that. [Ellen White was not a wallflower. She spoke her mind when necessary.] This is the light that has been given me in regard to these things.
>
> Here are children that are quick. There are children 5 years old that can be educated as well as many children 10 years old,

as far as capabilities are concerned, to take in the mother's matters and subjects.

Ellen White agreed that perhaps another room would have to be added to the school building, and declared, "Every one of us ought to feel a responsibility to provide that room." She followed by giving reasons for her advice:

> those mothers that want to keep their children at home, and are fully competent and would prefer to discipline them themselves, why, no one has any objection to that. They can do that. But provision is to be made so that the children of all that have any connection with this food factory and sanitarium and these things that are being carried on here, should be educated. We must have it stand to reach the highest standards. . . .
>
> I say, these little children that are small ought to have education, just what they would get in school. They ought to have the school discipline under a person who understands how to deal with children in accordance with their different temperaments. They should try to have these children understand their responsibilities to one another, and their responsibility to God. They should have fastened in their minds the very principles that are going to fit them for the higher grade and the higher school. . . .
>
> He wants this education to commence with the little ones. If the mother has not the tact, the ingenuity, if she does not know how to treat human minds, she must put them under somebody that will discipline them and mold and fashion their minds.
>
> Now, have I presented it so that it can be understood?"

W. C. White also attended that meeting. He explained that his interest in the situation was a broad one. He was concerned that consistent policies and curriculum be adopted as church schools were being established across the land and throughout the world. He stated:

> My interest in this school lies in the fact that it is our privilege to set a pattern. The successes and failures and the

rulings of this school will affect our church schoolwork throughout California and much farther, because of Sister Peck's long experience as a teacher, and her work with you, Mother, in helping to prepare the book on education. All these things have put this school where it is a city set on a hill.

This is how Ellen White summed up the meeting:

> We must educate our children so that we can come up to the gates of the city and say, "Here am I, Lord, and the children that Thou hast given me." We must not come up without our children to hear the words, "Where is My flock, My little flock, that I gave you—that beautiful flock that I gave you, where are they?" And we reply they have been left to drift right into the world, and so they are unfitted for heaven. What we want is to fit them for heaven so we can present the little flock to God, and say, "I have done my best."

"No statement was published at the time, but the discussion in this meeting helped to establish a pattern that guided parents who were not so situated that they could teach their children at home till they were 8 or 10. Their children's needs for a Christian elementary education could consistently be met" if church members and parents worked together.

So what did we learn here in this little school board meeting? First, God wants us to use common sense—biblical statements and Ellen White's writings are understood correctly only when time, place, and circumstances are considered. Second, Ellen White was not a spineless bystander in church affairs. Third, Ellen White's counsel is as relevant, as up-to-date as the six o'clock news. Fourth, it is always safest to listen to Ellen in most any circumstance where moral clarity and common sense is needed. "Believe His prophets!"

Chapter 21

Two Ladies Buy a Sanitarium— Origin of Paradise Valley Sanitarium

*I*n 1900, Ellen White returned to America after living in Australia for nine years. Many at age seventy-three would have retired— but not Ellen. Her mind was full of what could be done in southern California.

In the spring of 1902, Dr. T. S. Whitelock in San Diego had discovered a sanitarium property that had been vacant for years. A severe drought in southern California had greatly affected tourism and many businesses. A four-story, thirty-eight-bed institution on twenty acres of land could be bought for $20,000, a fraction of the original cost. In September, the mortgage holder reduced the price to $12,000.

On October 13, 1902, Ellen wrote that she was instructed that there would be "properties for sale on which buildings are already erected that could be utilized for our work, and that such properties will be offered to us at must less than their original cost."[1]

But no money was available—and certainly not $12,000—from the local conference of about 1,100 members with a debt of $40,000. But Ellen kept her eye on the property. A few months later, the mortgages were offered to the church for $8,000. In January 1904, Dr. Whitelock visited the property again. While he was at the property, a woman drove up and said that she spoke for the mortgage holder who wanted the church to make an offer. Then she said that perhaps $6,000 would close the deal.

But still no money in sight. But "when word reached Ellen White" at Elmshaven in northern California, she immediately "consulted with a close friend, Josephine Gotzian, and then telegraphed Dr. Whitelock to offer $4,000 for the mortgages," which was accepted on January 27, 1904. "The . . . property now belonged to Adventists, but not to the Southern California Conference."

This is how Ellen described the property:

> Here was a well-constructed, three-story building . . . with broad verandas, standing upon a pleasant rise of ground, and overlooking a beautiful valley. Many of the rooms are large and airy. . . . Besides the main building, there is a good stable, and also a six-room cottage, which can be fitted up for helpers. The property is conveniently located, being less than seven miles from San Diego, and about a mile from the National City post office. There are twenty-two acres of land. About one half of this had once been planted to fruit trees, but during the long drought that this country has suffered, all the trees died except the ornamental trees and shrubbery around the buildings, and about seventy olive trees on the terraces. . . . I never saw a building offered for sale that was better adapted for sanitarium work. If this place were fixed up, it would look just like places that have been shown me by the Lord.

How did the two women come up with four thousand dollars? "Ellen White . . . borrowed her $2,000 share . . . from the St. Helena Bank at 8 percent interest. Mrs. Gotzian provided the other $2,000." And together they "clasped hands in an agreement to unite in helping to purchase the Potts Sanitarium."[2] They had no thought of making money on their speculation; "they purchased it only to hold it until the business could be organized and the conference could take control."

Soon a handful of men and women began to restore the building that had been vacant for more than a dozen years. The main building was repaired, electricity was installed, fourteen rooms were furnished with high-quality furniture that was purchased at very low prices from several wealthy families who were leaving the area because of the long drought.

In spite of the miraculous price and ideal building, the property was not usable. The intrepid manager, E. R. Palmer, described the water situation: "The twenty-acre tract of land on which the building stands was as dry as the hills of Gilboa, with only a remote prospect for water underground." But "Palmer and his fellow workers knew from their contacts with Ellen White that it was in the providence of God that the institution had been bought. They were confident that God would find a way to meet their needs. Still, through the summer of 1904 they" watched the trees wither and die from the drought, which had already lasted more than eight years.

Even Ellen White wrote about the trees: "The poor, drying up, dying trees are beseeching us by their appearance for refreshing streams of water." And so Ellen White went into action and "recommended that Palmer obtain the services of a good Adventist well digger of her acquaintance, Salem Hamilton, who was then living in Nebraska. Accordingly, he was called west to dig the well. As Palmer related:

> With what anxiety we surveyed the ground and tried the wizard water stick and discussed the possibilities. . . .
>
> Finally we chose a place and began digging down through the dry earth where the dust flew more than twenty feet below the surface.

They selected a site just below the institution, and they began to dig.

Ellen White traveled south from Elmshaven, "arriving at the Potts property on Monday, November 7. Hamilton had reached a depth of eighty feet"—all hand dug! "From day to day she listened with interest to reports of progress, and frequently talked with Hamilton. One day she asked, 'What are you going to do, Brother Hamilton?'

" 'I have a question to ask you,' he answered. 'If you will answer that, I will give you my answer. Did the Lord tell you to buy this property?'

" 'Yes! Yes!' Ellen White replied. 'Three times I was shown that we should secure this particular property.'

" 'All right,' Mr. Hamilton said, 'I have my answer. The Lord would not give us an elephant without providing water for it to drink.' " And he kept on digging.

"By now he was well past the eighty-foot level and . . . no sign of moisture. But one day Hamilton thought he heard the sound of a stream of water in the gravel at the bottom of the well. When Palmer visited the site and looked down the well . . . Hamilton called up, 'Mr. Palmer, would you be afraid to come down? I think there is water not far away.' Palmer did go down, and he heard it distinctly, 'like the tinkle of a bell or the sound of a small waterfall in the depths of a forest,' " he said.

"Hamilton had tunneled in one direction, but to no avail. He now tunneled in another direction and with a vigorous blow his pick broke through the clay into a fine stream of water as large as a man's arm. The well quickly began to fill. There wasn't even time to get all the tools out. That night the water rose fifteen feet in the well.

"Excitedly E. R. Palmer hastened to Ellen White's room to announce the good news." The next day she wrote to her grandchildren:

> Yesterday morning Brother Palmer came to my room in company with your father . . . and told us there was fifteen feet of water in the well. This morning there is twenty feet of water and their tools at the bottom of the well. I cannot express to you how glad we all are made. Plenty of water for all purposes! This cannot be estimated by gold or by silver. Water means life. . . . The Lord has answered all our expectations, and we shall have reason for thanksgiving. . . . I want to praise the Lord with heart and soul and will.

Because of immediate interest from the surrounding community, patients began arriving before the hospital was officially open.

At first, housing hadn't even been prepared for staff nurses, who initially lived in tents. But a remarkable and great hospital was born.

Today, Paradise Valley Hospital has a 237-bed capacity with all the specialties of a modern hospital including a heliport. All this grand history because of a little lady who saw what others could not see and others who trusted with their lives in what Ellen White saw. Even a well for water was not beneath the attention of the Lord's messenger.

[1]Letter 157b, 1902.
[2]Letter 97, 1904.

Chapter 22

"Take Action at Once"— The Miracle of Loma Linda

*I*n 1905 Ellen White was seventy-eight years old, but *retirement* was not a word in her vocabulary. Or in the vocabulary of other church leaders, such as Stephen Haskell and John Loughborough. Ellen already had much to do with the establishment of two Adventist health centers in southern California—one at Paradise Valley (1904), near San Diego, and another in Glendale (1904), near Los Angeles. Without her vision and leadership, those two institutions, both still in operation today, would probably never have seen the light of day.

And God had additional plans for Adventist medical work in southern California. For some time before her journey to attend the 1905 General Conference session in Washington, D.C., Ellen White's thoughts "had been repeatedly called to the Redlands-Riverside-San Bernardino area . . . as a place where the church should have a sanitarium . . . the third . . . in southern California.

"Incredible as it sounded to 1,400 church members in the local conference and their leaders who had been warned not to go further into debt, God's messenger" wrote these instructions to J. A. Burden, manager of the Glendale Sanitarium: "Redlands and Riverside have been presented to me as places that should be worked. . . . Please consider the advisability of establishing a sanitarium in the vicinity of these towns.

"In response . . . a committee was appointed to look for such a site. They felt" that the Loma Linda resort hotel was an appropriate property, but the price tag of $85,000 was too much to consider. But by April 1, the price had been lowered, and the hotel could be bought for $45,000.

"On . . . May 4, when the eastbound train stopped at the Los Angeles station, a few of the brethren, including Elder Burden, boarded the car to tell Sister White about Loma Linda. She was immediately interested and excitedly urged, 'Look up all the particulars and write me at once in Washington.' "

Three days after she reached Washington, Friday, May 12, the promised letter was placed in Ellen White's hands.

"She read it aloud to her son W. C. White:

Dear Sister White: While on the train at Los Angeles, we spoke to you of a property for sale near Redlands which seemed to be well adapted for sanitarium purposes. . . . I am sending you a little pamphlet that contains a few views and a brief description of the property, but words and pictures can but faintly describe its beauty. It is simply ideal and grand for a sanitarium.

The buildings are in excellent condition, well furnished, heated with steam heat, and lighted with electricity. Everything is complete to begin business at once. The main building has forty-six rooms, and there are four cottages having four rooms each, with bath and toilet. Three of these cottages have four porches each, with broad windows, so that beds can be wheeled right out on the porch, and patients can sleep in the open air. There is another beautiful building—a two-story cottage of nine rooms, with bath and toilet. Another building which has been used as a recreation pavilion, and has four nice rooms, would make a fine gymnasium and chapel.

There are barns and sheds, and a house for the workmen. There are ten acres of good bearing orange orchard, fifteen acres of alfalfa, eight acres of apricots, plums, and almonds. The rest of the grounds are beautifully laid out in lawns, drives, and walks, there being more than a mile of cement walk. The principal buildings are on a beautiful knoll about 125 feet above the valley. The main building is surrounded with pepper-wood trees from thirty to forty feet high.

There are five horses, four cows, 150 chickens, thirty-five turkeys, some hogs, farm implements, buggies, carriages, and wagons.

The place has an ample supply of water from the mountains. An artesian well, which has a good pumping plant, yields an abundance of water, if for any reason the mountain water should fail. The water is piped all over the seventy-six acres.

The place cost the present owners $150,000. They have tried to run it as a tourist hotel, but it was a failure, and they lost money, so it was closed the first of April. The stockholders are financially embarrassed, and have ordered the property sold for $40,000. The furnishings alone in the buildings cost $12,000, and have been used for only about two years and a half.

A number of us went to see the place today, and we were deeply impressed that this is the place which the Lord has shown you, near Redlands and Riverside, in which sanitarium work should be carried on. It is five miles from Redlands.

The question is, what shall we do? We must act at once, for the company is anxious to sell, and there are others who want it. . . .

We do not wish to move hastily, and we should like to hear from you and the brethren in Washington who have gone from this field, as to how you and they feel about the matter. I wish that if it is at all possible you would take the matter up in council with them, and have them wire us. I do not know how long we can hold the offer open, but will try to do so until we hear from you. I think that those here who are considering the matter feel such a strong conviction that we should have the place that they will pay down a deposit, even if we lose it, rather than let the property pass out of our hands before we can hear from the brethren in Washington.

How I wish that you could have stopped off and seen the property while on your way to the conference; but it may be that you can return this way and see it then. I hope that you can send us some counsel as soon as you receive this letter.

Wishing you much of the blessing of the Lord in the conference, I am, Yours in the work, J. A. Burden.

"When she finished reading, she told Willie that she believed the place was the one that had been presented to her several years ago.

"She later wrote that the description given by Brother Burden answered in every respect to that of places she had been instructed would be opened to the church, at prices below their original cost. The terms offered Elder Burden were $5,000 down and like amounts in August . . . September . . . and December . . . making $20,000. The remaining $20,000 would come due in three years." How could they raise the money? The Southern California Conference was heavy in debt, and the General Conference, too, was facing overwhelming financial problems.

" 'We must take action at once,' Ellen White told her son.

" 'Willie,' she queried, 'Will you do as I ask?'

" 'I usually do,' he responded.

"Then came her request, 'I want you to send a telegram to Elder Burden to secure the property at once.'

"As Willie was leaving the room to send the telegram, she called him back and extracted a promise to send the telegram immediately, before taking counsel with anyone regarding the matter.

"He promised, and the telegram was sent." Ellen felt deep conviction that Loma Linda was the place God wished His people to have. Later, "she explained her instruction to W. C. White as follows, 'I did not consult with anyone, because I thought this would hinder us, and I believed that we could carry the matter forward without putting the burden on the conference.'

"Friday's telegram was followed by a letter to Elder Burden on Sunday, May 14, which opened:

Your letter has just been read. I had no sooner finished

reading [your letter] than I said, 'I will consult no one; for I have no question at all about the matter.' . . . Secure the property by all means, so that [it] can be held, and then obtain all the money you can and make sufficient payments to hold the place. This is the very property that we ought to have. Do not delay; for it is just what is needed. . . . We will do our utmost to help you raise the money. I know that Redlands and Riverside are to be worked, and I pray that the Lord may be gracious, and not allow anyone else to get this property instead of us. . . .

Here is the word of the Lord. Open up every place possible. We are to labor in faith, taking hold of a power that is pledged to do large things for us. We are to reach out in faith in Los Angeles and in Redlands and Riverside.

"Through the next three weeks letters and telegrams . . . crisscrossed the continent. Southern California Conference officers, after counseling with union conference leaders, telegraphed that the conference could take no responsibility in the matter."

From where would the funds come? "On Thursday, May 25, Elder Burden and a close friend, Elder R. S. Owen, a Bible teacher at the San Fernando school, took the inter-urban electric car down the coast to call on a farmer who was thought to have some means. He lived about a mile and a half from the car stop. When they got to his cabin, no one was at home. . . . The two men returned to the car stop and waited.

"It was dark now, and as the inter-urban car sped toward them, they failed to signal it for a stop. . . . There would be a two-hour wait for another car, so the men went back to the cabin, which now had a light in it. Finding the farmer, his wife, and daughter, they introduced themselves and soon explained their mission. Elder Burden reports that as the telegram from Mrs. White and the letters that followed were read to the farmer, he suddenly exclaimed, 'Praise the Lord!'

"He had been praying that the Lord would send someone to buy his place. It had been sold a few days before and now he was ready to make available $2,400 for the Loma Linda enterprise. The next day Elder Burden phoned the representative of the Loma Linda Association [owners of the hotel] that he was ready to do business. The $1,000 was paid, and work was begun on a contract. . . . Four thousand dollars more had to be on hand by June 15 to make up the first payment of $5,000 or the deposit would be lost. . . .

"Travel plans called for [Ellen White and her son Willie] to reach Redlands at 10:00 A.M. Monday, June 12. Local and union conference workers would come out from Los Angeles and meet them at Loma Linda. A great deal depended on this meeting." If the purchase were not approved, Elder Burden would lose the borrowed $1,000 given to bind the contract.

When Ellen White saw the main building, she said, "Willie, I have been here before."

" 'No, Mother,' he replied, 'you have never been here.'

" 'Then this is the very place the Lord has shown me,' she said, 'for it is all familiar.'

"Ellen White turned to one of the ministers and declared, 'We must have this place. We should reason from cause to effect. The Lord has not given us this property for any common purpose.'

"As they looked over grounds and buildings, she said again and again, 'This is the very place the Lord has shown me.' "

While touring the buildings, Ellen commented, "This building will be of great value to us. A school will be established here. Redlands will become a center as also will Loma Linda. Battle Creek is going down. God will reestablish His medical work at this place."

But, "in spite of the evidences of God's leading . . . the group facing such a stupendous project was unready to come to any decision. The financial problems loomed too large.

"So before taking any steps it was felt that the matter should be placed before the Los Angeles Carr Street Church, the largest in the conference. The meeting was called for ten o'clock the next day."

Ellen "did not meet with the conference committee that evening, but there it was argued that if a hundred businessmen and physicians, with all their resources, had failed in their Loma Linda project, what should lead the church group to think they could succeed?

Thus with four days remaining until June 15, when the first payment was due, the committee adjourned to await the meeting called in Los Angeles the next day.

"By 10:00 A.M. . . . the church on Carr Street was crowded. Sister White reviewed what had been revealed to her of the medical missionary work that should be carried forward in southern California. She told the audience that Loma Linda recalled to her mind visions of properties that ought to be secured for sanitarium work. The church members voted in favor of securing the property for a sanitarium.

"However, the officers of the Southern California Conference felt that more than one church should be heard from before the conference could" sponsor the project. They decided that delegates from churches throughout the conference would meet on June 20 to make a decision.

In the meantime, the payment of $4,000 would come due on June 15. "The farmer down the coast had provided $2,400. Brother Burden talked with a sister, Belle Baker. She could see no reason to hesitate and said she would put up $1,000. 'You may lose it,' Burden suggested. 'I'll risk it,' she replied.

"Then Burden conferred with his friend, R. S. Owen. 'I don't have the money,' Owen declared, 'but I'll mortgage my house for it.' . . . The June payment was made on schedule.

"Five days later, on June 20, the constituency of the Southern California Conference met. They were faced with the matter of whether Loma Linda should be purchased, and if so, whether it would be operated 'by private corporation or by the conference assuming the financial responsibility of the enterprise.' Ellen White was on hand for the meeting. She spoke for more than an hour about what should be done in southern California and urged the securing of the Loma Linda property. . . . She declared, 'This is the very property that we ought to have.'

"Still, the leading officers of the Southern California Conference hesitated. How, with the heavy debt on the conference, could they become further involved in securing properties and starting sanitariums? . . .

"Then Elder G. A. Irwin, the newly elected General Conference vice-president, rose to speak. He was on a mission to California, and while passing through Los Angeles had been urged to visit Loma Linda. He had just that morning come from there; he now spoke in favor of securing that institution. He rehearsed a number of incidents" in the past in which workers and church members had followed Mrs. White's counsel, and, as a result, God had blessed the projects with success.

"The audience listened attentively as Elder Irwin spoke with measured words:

> Although the conference is heavily in debt, I believe it to be to the glory of God that the conference should assume this responsibility.

"Elder Irwin's speech . . . turned the tide. The constituency voted unanimously in favor of securing the Loma Linda property and opening a third sanitarium in southern California. Cash and pledges totaling $1,100 were offered in support of the action. The enthusiastic response of a new church member, the daughter of Gen. Harrison Gray Otis, founder of the Los Angeles *Times*, who promised to give $10,000 if and when she could get the money released from another commitment, gave encouraging support. . . .

"But as the days came and went, the nagging question remained: From where would the $5,000 come for the [August] payment?

"Ellen White . . . was endeavoring to raise money. But there were no immediate responses." One suggestion seemed to offer a logical solution—sell some of the land! "Learning of this, Ellen White wrote to Burden on July 5: . . .

> I just thought to write you a few lines to assure you that not one foot of that land is to be sold to raise money. We will hire money at the bank rather than this shall be done."

Finally Wednesday, July 26, "dawned with still no money in sight. If the payment was not available by 2:00 P.M., the property and the initial $5,000 payment would be lost." The conference committee met that morning in Los Angeles under a heavy cloud.

"Some felt the circumstances justified the misgivings they had entertained from the start. Others, Elder Burden recounted, 'remembered the clear words that had come through the *Testimonies,* and refused to concede there should be failure.' As they reached out for deliverance, someone suggested that the morning mail had not yet come."

Elder Burden continued:

> Soon after this the postman was heard coming up the stairs. He opened the door and delivered the mail. Among the letters was one bearing the postmark Atlantic City, New Jersey.
>
> The letter was opened, and it was found to contain a draft for $5,000, just the amount needed for the payment.
>
> Needless to say, the feelings of those who had been critical were quickly changed. Eyes filled with tears, and one who had been especially critical was the first to break the silence. With trembling voice, he said, "It seems that the Lord is in this matter." "Surely He is," came a reply, "and He will carry it through to victory." The influence that filled the room that day hushed the spirit of criticism. It was as solemn as the judgment day.

Who sent that check from Atlantic City? A woman to whom Ellen White had appealed for help. Elder Burden pointed out:

> The Lord had put it into her heart to respond and to mail the letter just at the time when our faith had been tested almost to the limit, that it might be revived and strengthened.
>
> Soon we were at the bank window to pay in the $5,000. As the receipt was taken from the counter, a voice seemed to say to us, "See how nearly you missed that payment. How are you going to meet the next one, within a month?" In heart we answered, "It will surely come, even though we do not now know the source." We thanked God and took new courage in believing that the Lord was going before us.

"The August 26 payment of $5,000 was made on time, and a few days later the December 31 payment was also made. In fact, instead of taking three years to pay the second $20,000 of the purchase price, as allowed in the contract, it was taken care of within six months."

But securing the land for a sanitarium and a training school for nurses was only the beginning of Ellen White's vision for Loma Linda. What about a medical school for physicians?

In 1905, Mrs. White wrote, "In regard to the school, I would say, Make it all you possibly can in the education of nurses and physicians."

"In reporting to the readers of the *Review and Herald* on the dedication of Loma Linda on April 15, 1906, she announced:

> Loma Linda is to be not only a sanitarium, but an educational center. . . . A school is to be established here for the training of gospel medical missionary evangelists."

On "September 20, the Loma Linda College of Evangelists was opened, yet without a clear sense of direction. . . .

"On October 30, 1907, Ellen White . . . addressed students and faculty on the high standards that should characterize the educational features of the work. At the close of her presentation, Elder Burden addressed the question to her that was uppermost in his mind:

> I want to ask a question. Is this school that you have spoken of simply to qualify nurses, or is it to embrace also the qualification of physicians?

To this she replied,

> Physicians are to receive their education here."

When she learned that the school's leadership was proceeding along these lines but with the plan to provide acceptable two-year training at Loma Linda before sending the students to an accredited medical school elsewhere to finish their preparation, she had much to say.

"Elder Burden, on September 20, 1909, counseled with Ellen White at her home about this. He found that she was distressed with any plan that called for 'having medical students take some work at Loma Linda' and then 'get the finishing touches of their education from some worldly institution.' She exclaimed, 'God forbid that such a plan should be followed' and commented 'I must state that the light I have received is that we are to stand as a distinct, commandment-keeping people.' . . .

"As the steps were taken to secure a charter for medical education at Loma Linda, Ellen White on November 5, 1909, gave strong counsel:

> Some questions have been asked me regarding our relation to the laws governing medical practitioners. We need to move understandingly, for the enemy would be pleased to hedge up our work so that our physicians would have only a limited influence. Some men do not act in the fear of God, and they may seek to bring us into trouble by placing on our necks yokes that we could not consent to bear. We cannot submit to regulations if the sacrifice of principles is involved, for this would imperil the soul's salvation.
>
> But whenever we can comply with the law of the land without putting ourselves in a false position, we should do so. Wise laws have been framed in order to safeguard the people against the imposition of unqualified physicians. These laws we should respect, for we are ourselves protected from presumptuous pretenders. Should we manifest opposition to these requirements, it would tend to restrict the influence of our medical missionaries.

"On December 9, 1909, with the full approval of the General Conference Committee, a charter was secured under the laws of the State of California authorizing the College of Medical Evangelists to grant degrees in the liberal sciences, dentistry, and medicine."

Voting a charter overcame one hurdle. But that was only one step in actually establishing a medical school with all the costs involved. Key leaders on the West Coast were opposed because of the enormous costs.

"At the session of the Pacific Union Conference in late January, 1910, held at Mountain View, the future of medical education conducted by Seventh-day Adventists was in the balance."

Not only were key leaders not convinced, but there was also disagreement about how to interpret the term *medical education*. Conference leadership did not feel free to recommend such an enterprise before first satisfying themselves that they correctly interpreted Ellen White's instruction. So "on Tuesday, January 25, it was decided to make a specific inquiry of Ellen White . . . :

Dear Sister White: We have read the testimonies, as far as we have seen them, that you have given concerning Loma Linda, and the establishment of a medical school in connection with the work at that place. As far as we know, our people are anxious to carry out the light that the Lord has given; but there is a difference of opinion between us in regard to what you mean when you use the term, 'a medical school.' . . .

Her reply came on Thursday morning, January 27, in the clearest language.

The light given me is, We must provide that which is essential to qualify our youth who desire to be physicians, so that they may intelligently fit themselves to be able to stand the examinations required to prove their efficiency as physicians. They should be taught to treat understandingly the cases of those who are diseased, so that the door will be closed for any sensible physician to imagine that we are not giving in our school the instruction necessary for properly qualifying young men and young women to do the work of a physician. Continually the students who are graduated are to advance in knowledge, for practice makes perfect.

The medical school at Loma Linda is to be of the highest order, because those who are in that school have the privilege of maintaining a living connection with the wisest of all physicians, from whom there is communicated knowledge of a superior order. And for the special preparation of those of our youth who have clear convictions of their duty to obtain a medical education that will enable them to pass the examinations required by law of all who practice as regularly qualified physicians, we are to supply whatever may be required, so that these youth need not be compelled to go to medical schools conducted by men not of our faith. Thus we shall close a door that the enemy will be pleased to have left open; and our young men and young women, whose spiritual interests the Lord desires us to safeguard, will not feel compelled to connect with unbelievers in order to obtain a thorough training along medical lines. (Signed) Ellen G. White."

When the committee presented their detailed plan for the medical school to the full session, I. H. Evans, vice president of the General Conference, spoke:

I am deeply interested in what has been read to us tonight from the Spirit of Prophecy. The question before the meeting is one of great importance, and needs most careful consideration from every standpoint.

The establishment of a medical school has been under consideration for several years by some of our leading brethren. Not a few of our men have believed that we should have such a school. They have hesitated to establish a school, because of their lack of experience in operating such an enterprise, and because they did not know where to secure either the teachers or the money with which to carry forward the same.

When the statement from Sister White is read, I am sure that the majority of our brethren will feel as we feel tonight—

that the Lord has spoken, and we will obey. To some, this counsel from Sister White may come as a trial of their faith; to others, I am sure the words spoken will seem God-given and timely. Oftentimes, the light God has sent to His people has seemed to be foolishness to those who did not view things as Heaven views them.

Now if we always were wise-hearted, and saw everything as the Lord would have us view it, there would be no need of further light through the Spirit of Prophecy; but we are mortal, and our vision is limited, and we often see things in a perverted light. Because of our lack of clear perception, the Lord in mercy speaks to His people through the Spirit of Prophecy. He has had to do this in the past, and we may well hope that He may long continue speaking to us concerning our duty and the needs of His cause. . . .

I cannot think of a single enterprise that has been started by the instruction of the Spirit of Prophecy, that has not worked out for the best good of the Lord's work. Many times we have been told to move forward, when the Red Sea seemed before us, and the mountains on either side; but every time we have accepted the instruction and stepped cheerfully forward, the Lord has made plain a pathway in which we could walk, and we have found not only prosperity to the cause of God, but we have found our own hearts nurtured in the Lord. . . .

We have before us tonight a plain, straightforward statement from Sister White, in regard to the establishment of a medical school. There is no guesswork about it; there is no equivocation; there is no false construction that need be put upon these words. The question is, Will we follow the counsel given? Do we intend to obey what the Lord has said to us in regard to the establishment and maintenance of a medical school? . . .

Someone may say, "The time is most inopportune." But the question is, When the Lord reveals to us His desire that we shall establish a medical school, and do it soon, is the time inopportune for doing such a work? I can conjure up many reasons why at this time we are ill-prepared to establish and operate a medical school. It is not hard for any man to say that we have not the money at hand. Any man need not be very wise to say, "We do not know where we shall get medical men trained and qualified to take up this work. But the question is, Will we establish this medical school, when the Lord has indicated so plainly our duty? I believe, brethren, if we step forward in the fear of God, and make an effort to establish this school, the Lord will help us and make the way clear I believe we shall see light, more and more, as we advance by faith, in accordance with the words of counsel that have come to us through the servant of the Lord."

That speech summed up the faith and commitment of the Adventist movement—the same faith and commitment that had emerged sixty years before when the future seemed even more daunting. Where would Loma Linda University be today without the courage and vision-directed insights of Ellen White?

Historian Richard Utt said it well: "The rise of Loma Linda University was not so much fraught with the inevitable as with the impossible. That the feat was accomplished at all was due to a rare recipe of faith, works, and struggle, liberally laced with the improbable, the miraculous, and the heroic."

Chapter 23

"The Lord Forbids . . ."— The Saving of Boulder Sanitarium

*T*he Boulder (Colorado) Sanitarium crisis during 1905 is a case study in how an institution's mission is to take precedence over the institution's viability as a mere financial enterprise. In the case of the Boulder Sanitarium, church leaders viewed the struggling institution as a financial problem to be solved by using secular business practices, while Ellen White saw a bigger picture that included mission:

> By the work of our sanitariums, suffering is to be relieved and health restored. People are to be taught how, by carefulness in eating and drinking, they may keep well. Christ died to save men from ruin. Our sanitariums are to be His helping hand, teaching men and women how to live in such a way as to honor and glorify God. If this work is not done by our sanitariums, a great mistake is made by those conducting them.

Boulder Sanitarium, established in 1895 by Seventh-day Adventists, was built with money borrowed from the General Conference Association, money that came from funds invested by Adventists at low interest rates. The cost of the sanitarium was not to exceed $30,000, but, like so many projects, it ran over budget to $75,000. The plan was that "the organization making the investment in the Sanitarium would control it, and that the earnings of the institution would not only meet running expenses but in time repay the" church members who invested personal funds.

But that is not how it turned out. Control of the sanitarium "was transferred to the . . . Kellogg-controlled International Medical Missionary Association. The General Conference was given a note for $45,000 in return for its investment of $75,000. Officials of the Colorado Conference were dropped from the board. For years the institution struggled financially. . . .

"These were the circumstances when at the General Conference of 1905 in Washington, D.C.," an Adventist physician offered to purchase the institution for $50,000. For some time, this physician had been operating a competing institution only half a mile from the Boulder Sanitarium. It operated "with less discipline, lower standards, and higher employee remuneration," along with one significant lifestyle difference—the patients and guests were served meat.

"During the months preceding the General Conference session, [the physician] had succeeded in making friends of the members of the Colorado Conference committee who had been left off the Boulder Sanitarium board. Taking all factors into consideration, he expected to" purchase the Boulder Sanitarium for $50,000. And to many leaders, tired of the financial struggle, the doctor's offer seemed reasonable.

When Ellen White learned of these plans, she went before the General Conference session on Monday, May 29, vigorously protesting the proposed sale of Boulder Sanitarium. Her message was based not only on the physician's proposal but also on a vision given to her after she had arrived in Washington, D.C.

"Recently," she said, "the question has been raised, what shall we do with the Colorado Sanitarium?" Ellen then discussed the situation: "The light given me has been that the plans followed in the building up of this institution were not altogether in accordance with the mind and will of God. Too much money was invested in the building."

However, Ellen "pointed out that the solution . . . was not in selling and getting out, but in making the institution a success in spite of the problems. More than money was at stake:

> After the investment has been made, the buildings erected, and our workers have gone in there, and wrestled and wrestled

to make the work a success, and the Sanitarium has accomplished much good, shall we turn over the place to private parties? After the workers have wrestled all these years, shall those now connected with it give it up, and say they are beaten? We cannot have it so. No such representation of our work is to be made before the world."

Ellen was positive about the institution's future: "God wants us never to do such a thing as to part with the Boulder Sanitarium. This institution will yet do its work, and will do it well." She then stated that it was not in God's plan that a *second* medical institution should be operated in Boulder. "There were plenty of places a physician could go to establish another sanitarium"—but not in Boulder and not by this physician!

Another factor made the situation even more complicated: "Those carrying the responsibilities at the Sanitarium knew nothing prior to the General Conference session of the proposition that the institution be sold. When they learned what was going on, and that the president of the conference was a party to it, they were shocked" and felt betrayed. Not a pleasant time for anyone at this point.

Ellen White wrote a private letter to this enterprising physician:

You could not have properly considered the results upon others, or you would not have established a sanitarium where you are now located. Your management in this matter has not pleased the Lord. . . .

Why was our Boulder Sanitarium established? Was it not to teach health reform, and use rational methods in the treatment of disease? . . . if your institution gives indulgence to meat-eating and various other appetites, then is not its influence against the sanitarium already established, where the principles of health reform are upheld? . . .

But by the location of another sanitarium so nearby, the principles of which are in some respects quite different from those of the Boulder Sanitarium, difficulties will be presented which should not exist.

Ellen's straight testimony at that May conference in Washington, D.C., slowed any action to sell the sanitarium. But not all in Colorado were convinced. Another plan was introduced—"the proposition of establishing a new sanitarium . . . in Canon City, 100 miles to the south of Boulder. . . . The chief attraction was newly developed artesian wells with mineral water thought to be of curative value."

The planners did their work well. The Denver papers of August 5 carried the story of a new corporation that would open a general tourist sanitarium in Canon City. Who were the incorporators? Two physicians, the country treasurer, a banker, and the president of the Colorado Conference. First on the list of the proposal as it appeared in the newspapers was "the founding of a general tourist sanitarium." The rest of the land would be leased to manufacturing plants and other businesses, including cattle ranching. The promoters hoped to raise some $40,000. Where did they plan to get the money? From Seventh-day Adventists!

This public announcement discouraged the people trying to make the Boulder Sanitarium a success, and it led Ellen White to re-enter the picture. This is what Ellen wrote on August 10 to physicians and ministers in Colorado: "I have a message for the brethren who contemplate establishing a sanitarium at Canon City. The Lord forbids, at this time, any movement that would tend to draw to other enterprises the sympathy and support that are needed just now by the Boulder Sanitarium. This is a critical time for that institution." She urged that their attention and funds should be focused on Boulder Sanitarium until it was free from debt.

Now a new player entered the discussion. The Colorado camp meeting was scheduled for August 17–27 in Denver. "Elder G. A. Irwin, General Conference vice-president, was on the West Coast awaiting the arrival of his wife from Australia. . . . He was to attend the Colorado meeting as a General Conference representative and was fully aware of the confused and critical situation in that state. He asked Ellen White to let him have copies of what she had written from time to time about Boulder Sanitarium. He would take with him what he could, and other documents would be mailed to him in Denver.

"Ellen White was to leave August 10 for the Los Angeles camp meeting. Before leaving, she was up much of two nights writing and getting testimonies ready for Colorado. She and her staff assembled the materials, and the secretaries copied five key documents, which, after a careful final reading by Ellen White, were hastened by mail to Elder Irwin."

In her August 10 communication, Ellen dealt again very plainly with the three issues: (1) the need to turn the Boulder Sanitarium into a thriving medical institution; (2) the proposed purchase of the Boulder Sanitarium by the physician who ran the competing institution in Boulder; and (3) the plan to build the Canon City Sanitarium by developers who included the conference president. Elder Irwin received these new messages by mail in Denver—and he used them effectively.

"After the difficult Denver meeting, Elder Irwin wrote how he had dreaded that meeting, for 'there were so many conflicting interests to harmonize.' But, he reported, 'the testimonies . . . came just at the right time.' He first took the conference president aside . . . and read him the testimonies. . . . The president listened very attentively. . . . He had favored the transfer of Boulder Sanitarium to [the physician], and was also . . . in sympathy with the enterprise in Canon City. . . . But he accepted the counsel.

"Elder Irwin then talked" to others individually, and they conceded to Ellen White's counsel, "although it was clear that it was" a disappointment to them. Then, Elder Irwin read the messages from Ellen White "to the conference committee and then to all the workers of the Colorado Conference. With the workers committed, Elder Irwin took the matter to the whole body of believers assembled, where a vote was taken. There was not a dissenting vote." This was an amazing feat of Christian leadership by Elder Irwin.

The Lord's advice was accepted and followed. "The conference committee issued a statement, referring first to the counsel given, which 'met with a hearty general response on the part of our conference workers and conference delegates.' "

When Irwin reviewed the events that had taken place at the camp meeting, he noted that Ellen's counsel "seemed to cut directly across plans that were believed to be right and that accorded with the best judgment of those concerned." Nevertheless, when the conference workers received a clear message from the Lord, they willingly abandoned their own plans and accepted the instruction sent to them by the Lord's messenger.

Afterward, the conference committee realized that "in the reorganization of Boulder Sanitarium, it was now 'more than ever before a denominational institution.' Full support of the conference constituency was solicited."

Intervention by the Lord's messenger turned the Boulder Sanitarium into a thriving denominational institution. Her advice contradicted plans laid by powerful businessmen with good intentions. But the Lord's messenger was able to see more than the best of men could see. Still today, the Boulder Sanitarium episode is a reminder for church leaders and constituents that the mission of an institution, not its financial success, is the basis for its existence.

Chapter 24

The Shortest Testimony— Saving the Battle Creek Tabernacle

*T*he shortest testimony Ellen White ever gave was a telegram received by the pastor of the Battle Creek Tabernacle in early 1907 during the struggle over the ownership of that church building. It was not a cheery time for those involved.

For years the crisis had been developing over the ownership and control of this much-loved church, "which could comfortably seat 2,400 people, and 3,200 when opened fully." It was by far the biggest church in town.

Close by was the world-famous Battle Creek Sanitarium. By 1907, Dr. John Harvey Kellogg and his followers had wrested control of the sanitarium from the denomination, and now their attention was focused on taking over the largest church in the denomination (often known as the Dime Tabernacle). Strange as it may seem, most of the church trustees were inclined to support the sanitarium group's wishes.

In July 1906, a few months before the crisis came to a head, Ellen had written: "I have seen that the leaders in the medical work in Battle Creek will try to secure possession of the Tabernacle. Their scheming is so subtle that I greatly fear that this may be accomplished." Although no evidence at the time existed that such would take place, she wrote her son, Willie, that "it will require earnest effort to save the Tabernacle to the denomination."

For months the church had been without a pastor, probably because no one wanted to risk the stress. Finally, M. N. Campbell, thirty-two years old and just ordained, was chosen. Shortly after he moved to Battle Creek in November 1906, he discovered that the church's "charter had expired in 1892, fourteen years earlier, and the trustees had done nothing to renew it. He did his homework well, seeking legal advice and studying the steps that had to be taken to keep the Tabernacle" in the denomination.

However, most of the board members "were very favorable to Dr. Kellogg and Elder [A. T.] Jones. The new pastor made friends with the trustees" and talked with them about reincorporating the charter. "They talked it over and decided to do just that. The date was set for the legal meeting.

"But the agreement did not hold for long. When Campbell arrived home, the telephone rang. The trustees said that if they were to go through with [the meeting], A. T. Jones must have the right to take part in the legal meeting. Campbell's reply was a decided No!" Why? they asked. Because "Jones was not a member of the Battle Creek church, and he was not a man the church had confidence in. Other conditions were proposed that Campbell could not accept, and the trustees declared that the meeting they had agreed to would not be held. To this the young pastor responded, 'I'm here to tell you, my brother, that that meeting will be held.'

"But Campbell did not know how it could be done. . . . A day or two later the minutes of a board meeting of the Battle Creek Sanitarium in which the ownership of the Tabernacle was discussed fell into his hands." When Campbell confronted his church board with this documentation of their disloyalty, he gave them a choice: either go ahead and have the legal meeting to reincorporate the church, or have those minutes read to the congregation the following Sabbath.

"They quickly agreed to the legal meeting," voicing their fear that if the minister read those minutes, "We will have to move out of town. Campbell promised secrecy on the point if they would agree not to 'move a finger to interfere with the procedures to be taken to safeguard the Tabernacle.'

"But when the first legal meeting was held, every step possible was taken to delay . . . what had to be done. In all, five critical legal sessions were held, each freighted with uncertainties. Both Campbell and" George Amadon, an aged publishing house worker who came to Battle Creek in 1857 and a long-time church elder, "reported on the last and most crucial" meeting. "New articles of incorporation were to be voted and new trustees elected.

"A little time before the meeting, the pastor called a few of the leading brethren together for . . . prayer. 'They were all good, faithful men,' Campbell reported, 'but I don't know that I ever saw a set of men more scared. Old Brother Amadon, one of the finest Christians that ever lived, moaned, "If only Sister White were here, if only Sister White were here." '

"Campbell replied, 'Well, brother, she isn't. No use groaning over that. But we are here. We've got to handle this thing.'

"All of them knew Ellen White was in California, but Amadon continued, 'Oh, if only Sister White were here.'

"Ten minutes before the meeting was to open, a Western Union messenger came to the door and inquired: 'Is Mr. Campbell here?'

"Campbell said, 'Yes,' and reached out for the telegram addressed to him. Opening it he found this message: 'Philippians 1:27, 28. (Signed) Ellen G. White.'

"It was a testimony, her shortest testimony ever. Opening their Bibles to the reference given, they read:

> Let your conversation be as it becometh the gospel of Christ: that whether I come and see you, or else be absent, I may hear of your affairs, that ye stand fast in one spirit, with one mind striving together for the faith of the gospel; and in nothing terrified by your adversaries: which is to them an evident token of perdition, but to you of salvation, and that of God.

Elder Campbell later wrote:

> That settled the question. That was a communication from Sister White that we needed right at that moment. God knew we were holding that meeting, and that we had a group of

scared men, and that we needed help from Him, and so He gave us the message that came straight to us in the nick of time. It sounded pretty good to us.

"In spite of the fact that every conceivable step was taken by the opposition to block the work of reorganization, the meeting was conducted successfully and adjourned somewhat after 11:00 P.M. Elder Campbell read again at that meeting Ellen White's counsel to safeguard the Tabernacle. . . .

"The next morning George Amadon wrote to W. C. White at Elmshaven:

> With much joy I hastily pen you a few lines. Many thanks for the telegram. How appropriate was the scripture. Well, . . . it was half-past eleven before we got home. There was a persistent and unreasonable opposition to every step taken.

"Amadon reported that three fourths of the church congregation voted for the articles and bylaws.

"The Lord through His servant had sent warning messages" for many months. But nothing could have been more dramatic or timelier than that short telegram, Ellen's shortest testimony. Her timing was impeccable! "The Battle Creek Tabernacle was saved for Seventh-day Adventists." One more reason among many to trust the messenger of the Lord.